WHAT WE KNOW ABOUT
MATHEMATICS
TEACHING AND LEARNING

THIRD EDITION

Solution Tree | Press
McREL

Published by Solution Tree Press
555 North Morton Street
Bloomington, IN 47404

800.733.6786 (toll free) / 812.336.7700
FAX: 812.336.7790

email: info@solution-tree.com
solution-tree.com

Printed in the United States of America

14 13 12 11 10   1 2 3 4 5

FSC
Mixed Sources
Product group from well-managed
forests and other controlled sources
Cert no. SW-COC-002283
www.fsc.org
© 1996 Forest Stewardship Council

Library of Congress Cataloging-in-Publication Data

What we know about mathematics teaching and learning / McREL. -- 3rd ed.
    p. cm.
  Includes bibliographical references and index.
  ISBN 978-1-935249-95-5 (perfect bound) -- ISBN 978-1-935249-96-2 (library binding) 1. Mathematics--Study and teaching--United States. I. Mid-continent Research for Education and Learning (Organization)
  QA13.W43 2010
  510.71'073--dc22
                    2009052669

Solution Tree

Jeffrey C. Jones, CEO & President

Solution Tree Press

President: Douglas M. Rife

Publisher: Robert D. Clouse

Vice President of Production: Gretchen Knapp

Managing Production Editor: Caroline Wise

Copy Editor: Rachel Rosolina

Proofreader: Sarah Payne-Mills

Text and Cover Designer: Orlando Angel

McREL Research and Writing Team

The third edition of *What We Know About Mathematics Teaching and Learning* was produced by a team of mathematics educators and writers from Mid-continent Research for Education and Learning (McREL).

Project Manager
Linda Brannan

Editors
Vicki Urquhart
Kirsten Miller

Math Educators
Kathleen Dempsey
Heather Martindill

ELL Specialists
Jane Hill
Candace Hyatt

Librarian
Maura McGrath

Acknowledgments

The second edition of *What We Know About Mathematics Teaching and Learning* was produced by a team of mathematics educators and writers from McREL with support from external reviewers from the faculty of Metro State College of Denver and Colorado Online Learning: project manager and indexer—Linda Brannan; editor—Vicki Urquhart; writers and subject matter experts—Carmon Anderson, Kathleen Dempsey, and Matt Kuhn; reviewers—Ceri Dean, Brook Evans, Don D. Gilmore, and Jodi Holzman; librarian—Terry Young; graphics and layout—Jennifer Valentine and Natalie Voltes; cover art—Natalie Voltes.

The first edition was a collaborative publication of McREL, the Association of State Supervisors of Mathematics, and the National Network of Eisenhower Regional Consortia and Clearinghouse. It was produced in whole or in part with funds from the U.S. Department of Education National Eisenhower Mathematics and Science Programs Office of Educational Research and Improvement, under grant R168R950025–00. The team for the first edition included: editors—Jim Harper, Barbara Hicks, Nancy Kellogg, Alice Krueger, Carolyn Richbart, Lynn Richbart, John Sutton, Vicki Urquhart, and Janie Zimmer; writers and subject matter experts—Gary Appel, Malcolm Butler, Anne Collins, Ella-Mae Daniel, Elaine DeBassige D'Amato, Judy Florian, Fred Gross, Jodean Grunow, Carol Hanley, Clare Heidema, Bill Hopkins, Deb Jordan, Mozell Lang, Arlene Mitchell, Brett Moulding, Randi Peterson, Gwen Pollock, Linda Schoen, Sharon Stenglein, Jan Tuomi, and Jim Woodland; librarians—Linda Brannan, Norma Brown, and Terry Young; graphics and layout—Dawn McGill and Molly Drew; indexer—James Sucha.

Solution Tree Press would like to thank the following reviewers:

Suzanne Baker
Physics Teacher
Edward White High School
Jacksonville, Florida

Candace Barich
Fourth- to Fifth-Grade Teacher
South Colby Elementary
Port Orchard, Washington

Jennifer Bay-Williams
Associate Professor, Department of
   Teaching and Learning
University of Louisville
Louisville, Kentucky

David Berger
Math Teacher
Menomonie High School
Menomonie, Wisconsin

Abigail Chillemi
Math Teacher
Lincoln Middle School
Schiller Park, Illinois

Carrie S. Cutler
Lecturer, Department of Curriculum
   and Instruction
University of Houston
Houston, Texas

Patrick Flynn
Math Teacher
Olathe East High School
Olathe, Kansas

Alan Hack
Math Teacher
Northwestern Lehigh Middle School
New Tripoli, Pennsylvania

Alexander Kukushkin
Math Teacher
Golden Gate High School
Naples, Florida

Matt Larson
Math Curriculum Specialist
Lincoln Public Schools
Lincoln, Nebraska

Holly Neer
Fifth-Grade Teacher
Bryant Elementary
Oklahoma City, Oklahoma

Lisa Paffrath
First-Grade Teacher
Anthem School
Anthem, Arizona

Table of Contents

About McREL

Based in Denver, Colorado, McREL (Mid-continent Research for Education and Learning) is a nonprofit organization dedicated to its mission of making a difference in the quality of education and learning for all through excellence in applied research, product development, and service. For more than forty years, McREL has served as the federally funded regional educational laboratory for seven states in the U.S. heartland. Today, it provides services to an international audience of educators. Specifically, it offers a variety of services to help districts translate guidance from this book into results for students. To learn more, contact McREL at 1.800.781.0156 or info@mcrel.org.

Preface to the Third Edition

Many good intentions have gone into ambitious education reform goals, including those ratified by the U.S. Congress in 1985 and embodied in the No Child Left Behind (NCLB) Act of 2002. Despite these noble efforts, as of 2009 the United States has not made substantial progress toward the goal of becoming first in the world in mathematics and science education. In international comparisons, U.S. students' overall mathematics and science achievement ranks behind nearly a dozen other nations. The Trends in International Mathematics and Science Study (TIMSS) from 1995 showed our third- and fourth-graders scoring above the international average but our twelfth-graders scoring well below. The TIMSS-repeat results released in 2007 for fourth- and eighth-graders show significant improvement. However, countries other than the United States have statistically higher rates of growth. In 2003, the Program for International Student Assessment (PISA) reported that fifteen-year-olds' performance in mathematics literacy and problem solving ranked lower than the average performance for most industrialized countries. Although the United States appears to be making some small gains, the question still remains: what more can be done to make a difference?

What We Know About Mathematics Teaching and Learning provides a starting place by summarizing educational research and surveys of best classroom practices and offering implications for improved teaching and learning. This resource is not intended to be a complete look at all educational research; it aims only to touch on each focus area and guide the user to resources for additional study. Classroom teachers and preK–12 administrators will find this resource useful for their own professional development; educators can use it to inform and inspire their students, and parents and the public can read about the intended and achieved results of educational practices. Effective reforms in mathematics education practice and policy will require the collaboration of all these stakeholder groups. They will need a common understanding of the current status of mathematics education and of the direction that the "Research and Ideas to Know About" sections indicate for improvement, and they will need to understand how they can help accomplish reform. We hope that this resource provides a foundation for greater understanding and reflection.

As the way we live, work, and learn changes, methods of doing and communicating mathematics continue to emerge and evolve. The level of mathematics needed for thoughtful citizenship is increasing along with the need for greater mathematical problem solving. Today's students must develop skills to manage and use knowledge to solve problems in the personal, social, and economic realms, not just in textbooks. They need to know how to access, evaluate, and use information, all skills that are part of mathematics literacy.

More and more we see demand building for basing educational practice on empirical evidence and solid research. Why is education research an essential, yet insufficient, foundation on which to build student achievement? In the classroom, the critical factor in a lesson's success (that is, whether the students actually learn something that matters) is the professional knowledge and creative ability of the teacher—specifically the teacher's ability to know and understand research and to translate it into practical classroom experience. Research by itself will not result in effective teaching and learning, nor will practice alone result in positive student outcomes. Critical to student success is teachers' knowledge of subject content, skill in implementing appropriate instructional strategies, use of appropriate assessment tools, and commitment to ensure equal opportunity to learn for all students. Little of this can be accomplished unless teachers are knowledgeable about new research and determined to implement its findings. Effective teaching, therefore, involves the practical application of new research and theory in a classroom environment.

Principles and Standards for School Mathematics (*PSSM*; also known as the National Council of Teachers of Mathematics, or NCTM, Standards), published in 2000, describes a vision of a mathematically powerful student and offers a set of goals for mathematics instruction—the basic skills and understandings students need to function effectively in the twenty-first century. It asserts that enhanced career opportunities exist for those who understand and can do mathematics. It further states that mathematics education should prepare all students, not just a select few, to use mathematics appropriately in their careers and their lives.

The National Mathematics Advisory Panel convened in 2006 to examine the best available scientific research and to recommend improvements in the mathematics education of U.S. children. The panel's final report, *Foundations for Success*, describes concrete steps that can be taken now to significantly improve mathematics education, but it views these steps only as a best start in a long process. The panel's recommendations included a long-range plan to improve the quality and quantity of research on effective mathematics education.

Our purpose in compiling this publication is to support reform of mathematics education and to bring the rich world of educational research and practice to preK–12 educators. Each question we address provides background information from the perspectives of research, followed by implications for improving classroom instruction. Each question concludes with a list of resources for further reading.

We recognize that both U.S. mathematics standards and *Foundations for Success* describe not only important curricular content, but also ways to reform all parts of the educational system to promote improved teaching and student achievement. Systemic reform purposefully revises and aligns all components of a system. The mathematics education system is complex, including components such as assessment, curriculum, equity, student outcome standards, teaching, professional development of teachers, stakeholder involvement, leadership, and policy. Although we do not address all of these topics in this publication, all are important in the context of systemic reform of mathematics education.

Because classroom teachers are mainly concerned with what works in their own classrooms, *What We Know About Mathematics Teaching and Learning* balances presenting research findings with drawing implications from the research. The background research and related documents for the questions we include are intentionally succinct. A full citation of all references, however, appears in the back of this resource. We encourage you to examine the primary source documents, delve into educational research, and apply the findings in your own classrooms.

Every person concerned with teaching and learning mathematics, whether a teacher, administrator, student of education, parent, community member, or member of the higher education community, will find useful information here. As the United States moves forward in mathematics education reform, it must apply lessons learned to achieve improved mathematics education for all students—a goal the nation cannot afford to ignore.

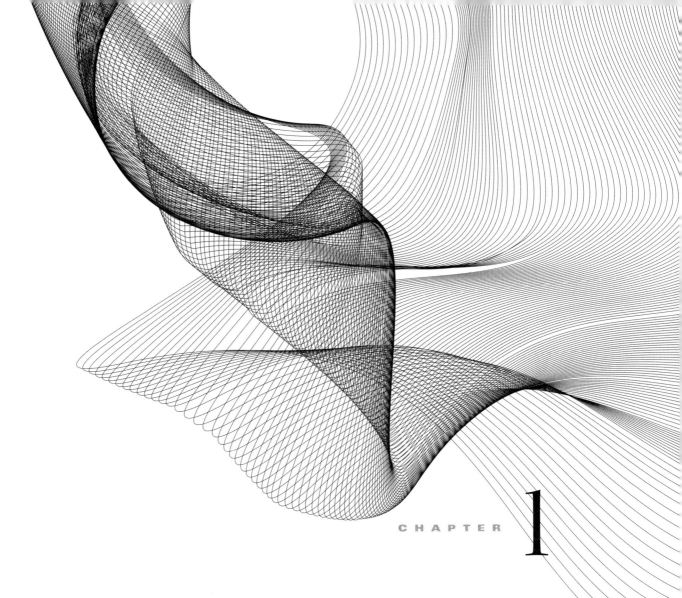

CHAPTER 1

Mathematics for All

All students can learn mathematics, and they deserve the opportunity to do so. The National Council of Teachers of Mathematics' *Principles and Standards for School Mathematics* sets forth mathematics literacy expectations for all students and describes what they are expected to learn. However, recognizing the diversity among American children, educators do not expect all students to learn the material in the same manner, with the same resources, or in the same time frame. The Equity Principle in *PSSM* states:

> All students, regardless of their personal characteristics, backgrounds, or physical challenges, must have opportunities to study—and support to learn—mathematics. Equity does not mean that every student should receive identical instruction; instead, it demands that reasonable and appropriate accommodations be made as needed to promote access and attainment for all students. (2000, p. 12)

To achieve "mathematics for all" will take a concerted effort from all stakeholders in our children's education. We must continue to make progress toward providing rich, well-supported learning environments that respond to the unique educational needs of every student. That is the goal of mathematics education reform.

What is equity, and how is it evident in mathematics classrooms?

Research and Ideas to Know About

An equitable mathematics program provides high-quality mathematics education for all students, in which they have access not only to quality mathematics courses and instruction, but also to the support they need to succeed in those courses. Equitable school programs must ensure that student differences in achievement are not based on race, ethnicity, gender, class bias, or physical disability. Some research suggests that access to and success in higher mathematics leads to greater financial opportunities; therefore, it is becoming an important civil rights issue in education.

Differences in mathematics achievement among various gender, income, and ethnic groups have been widely reported. For instance, while the National Research Council did not find significant differences between male and female students who had taken the same mathematics coursework, the achievement gap for minority learners continues to widen. The number of English language learners (ELLs) in classrooms across the United States is increasing, even in localities that had no ELLs just a few years ago. Furthermore, the field of special education has moved steadily toward the goal of inclusive instruction for students with disabilities.

Achievement in higher-level mathematics is a gatekeeper to success in higher education and in twenty-first-century careers. Research by the U.S. Department of Education indicates that the intensity and quality of the academic content and performance a student brings from secondary school to higher education is a major predictor of postsecondary degree attainment. Group achievement differences in mathematics can often be attributed to enrollment patterns or instructional strategies, leading some to believe that these differences are more of an opportunity gap than an achievement gap. Low-socioeconomic status (SES) students and minority students are half as likely to enroll in higher-level mathematics courses as high-SES white students. Low-SES students and those belonging to minority groups who took high school algebra and geometry attended college in percentages approximately equal to high-SES white students who had enrolled in the same high school courses. Research indicates that when low-income and minority students experience greater success in high school mathematics and science courses, the overall achievement gap between students of differing ethnic and socioeconomic groups diminishes.

Research findings also indicate that younger and lower-ability students can learn to employ the same strategies and skills for mathematical reasoning and thinking as those used by older and higher-ability students. Because different students learn in different ways, equal treatment for all students does not guarantee equal success. Teachers and counselors need to facilitate equal access to algebra, geometry, and higher-level mathematics courses.

> An equitable mathematics program provides high-quality mathematics education for all students.

Implications to Think About

To create an equitable classroom, teachers use various strategies to reach all students with high-quality content. These strategies include:

- Clearly identifying the knowledge students need to master

- Addressing different student needs and learning styles

- Encouraging active participation by all students

- Challenging all students by communicating high expectations and a deep belief in their capabilities

- Diagnosing where students are struggling to learn and providing appropriate instruction

- Embedding various assessment types throughout units of study

- Engaging all students in higher-order thinking skills (such as data analysis, synthesis of results, and evaluation of potential solutions)

- Helping students make meaningful connections among related mathematics concepts, across other disciplines (such as science or social studies), and with everyday experiences

- Providing continual academic support for student learning

- Using inclusive language in all classroom communication

- Engaging parents in student learning

Teachers need adequate knowledge of mathematics content and pedagogy to effectively address the needs of a diverse group of students. Teachers should regularly take advantage of content-specific professional development opportunities to enrich their content knowledge and to stay abreast of the latest teaching techniques.

The physical environment of the classroom should be interesting and inclusive for all students, with visible displays of student work and materials that show diverse groups of people involved in mathematics activities and careers. The context for instruction (that is, small or large groups) should invite all students to participate regardless of their current achievement levels.

The focus of an equitable mathematics program must be on student outcomes. Teachers and principals are responsible for all students' achievement; consequences for lack of student success fall not only on students, but also on teachers, principals, the school, and the family.

Resources for Learning More

Adelman, C. (1999). *Answers in the tool box: Academic intensity, attendance patterns, and bachelor's degree attainment.*

Evan, A., Gray, T., & Olchefske, J. (2006). *The gateway to student success in mathematics and science: A call for middle school reform—the research and its implications.*

Flores, A. (2007, November). "Examining disparities in mathematics education: Achievement gap or opportunity gap?"

Hambrick, A., & Svedkauskaite, A. (2005). *Critical issue: Remembering the child: On equity and inclusion in mathematics and science classrooms.*

Moses, R. P., & Cobb, C. E., Jr. (2001). *Radical equations: Math literacy and civil rights.*

National Council of Supervisors of Mathematics. (2008b, Spring). *Improving student achievement by leading the pursuit of a vision for equity.*

National Mathematics Advisory Panel. (2008). *Foundations for success: The final report of the National Mathematics Advisory Panel.*

National Research Council. (1989). *Everybody counts: A report to the nation on the future of mathematics education.*

Payne, R. K. (2005). *A framework for understanding poverty.*

Quiroz, P. A., & Secada, W. G. (2003). "Responding to diversity."

Schoenfeld, A. H. (2002, January–February). "Making mathematics work for all children: Issues of standards, testing, and equity."

Tennison, A. D. (2007, August). "Promoting equity in mathematics: One teacher's journey."

How do ability grouping and tracking affect student learning?

Research and Ideas to Know About

When addressing diverse student needs, teachers should consider the implications of assigning students to ability groups or tracks for mathematics instruction. Research suggests that these practices do not provide the same educational experience for all students. Equity for the student should be a foremost reference point for teacher reflection in addressing the complex issue of who should learn what mathematics and when.

Students deemed less capable experience less depth and breadth in school mathematics.

Studies suggest that student expectations vary according to assigned ability groups or tracks. Students deemed less capable experience less depth and breadth in school mathematics. Research indicates that the most experienced teachers are assigned to teach high-level classes, whereas teachers with the least experience and mathematical background are assigned to teach the lowest-performing mathematics students. Studies also reveal crucial differences in the kinds of instruction offered in different tracks. Instruction in the lower tracks tends to be fragmented, often requiring mostly memorization of basic facts and algorithms as well as worksheet completion. Although some higher-track classes share these traits, they are more likely to offer opportunities for making sense of mathematics, including discussion, writing, and applying mathematics to real-life situations.

Ability grouping and tracking rarely allow for upward movement when a student makes a developmental leap. Research shows that due to course filtering in the eighth grade, many students do not have access to rigorous high school mathematics classes. As a result, a conflict exists between the structure of academic ability groups or tracks and the potential academic and intellectual growth of struggling students who may be late bloomers.

An alternative to homogeneous strategies of ability grouping or tracking is mixed-ability or heterogeneous grouping for instruction. Heterogeneous instruction emphasizes a differentiated classroom approach in which teachers diagnose students' needs and design instruction based on their understanding of mathematics content by using various instructional strategies that focus on essential concepts, principles, and skills. Inherent in this practice is the opportunity for all students to receive quality mathematics instruction. As the demand for a more mathematically literate society continues, schools need to respond to this challenge and provide meaningful mathematics to all students all of the time.

Implications to Think About

To effectively teach students coming from a variety of previous mathematics learning experiences and successes, teachers should thoughtfully choose instructional strategies for working with de-tracked or heterogeneous groups. Each teacher must believe that all students can learn, although in different ways and at different rates.

These instructional elements have been shown to be effective for mixed-ability mathematics classes:

- *A meaningful mathematics curriculum*—This means providing contexts that give facts meaning, teaching concepts that matter, and framing lessons as complex problems.

- *An emphasis on interactive endeavors that promote divergent thinking within a classroom*—Students need to construct knowledge with peers (including safe opportunities to take risks on a regular basis), exchange ideas, and revise their understanding of mathematics.

- *Diversified instructional strategies that address the needs of all types of learners*—Embracing multiple intelligences means presenting information in various ways.

- *Assessment that is varied, ongoing, and embedded in instruction*—Performance assessments, a portfolio of growth and achievements, projects demonstrating the accompanying mathematics, and the opportunity to solve and report on complex problems in varied contexts will provide evidence of student learning.

- *Focused lesson planning*—Instead of emphasizing what the classroom teacher wants to teach, a focused lesson plan begins by understanding what students need to learn and assessing what they already know.

Employing these techniques will provide a rich classroom experience and an effective way to enhance mathematics learning for all students.

Resources for Learning More

Battista, M. T. (1994). "Teacher beliefs and the reform movement of mathematics education."

Lubienski, S. T. (2006). "Examining instruction, achievement, and equity with NAEP mathematics data."

Moses, R. P., & Cobb, C. E., Jr. (2001). *Radical equations: Math literacy and civil rights.*

Oakes, J. (2005). *Keeping track: How schools structure inequality.*

Rousseau, C., & Tate, W. F. (2003, Summer). "No time like the present: Reflecting on equity in school mathematics."

Tennison, A. D. (2007, August). "Promoting equity in mathematics: One teacher's journey."

Tomlinson, C. A. (1999). *The differentiated classroom: Responding to the needs of all learners.*

Tomlinson, C. A. (2003). *Fulfilling the promise of the differentiated classroom: Strategies and tools for responsive teaching.*

Tomlinson, C. A., & McTighe, J. (2006). *Integrating differentiated instruction and understanding by design: Connecting content and kids.*

How can schools facilitate students' opportunity to learn mathematics?

Research and Ideas to Know About

A basic definition of *opportunity to learn* (OTL) is the provision of various circumstances and conditions to promote learning. Teachers serve as the primary OTL gatekeeper. Although school counselors and other staff play important roles in facilitating OTL, it is mainly the teacher who ensures that opportunities exist.

Opportunity to learn is facilitated through classrooms that focus on higher-order thinking skills, problem solving, substantive conversation, and real-world contexts.

OTL components include the ability to take needed courses, access to a curriculum that meets content standards and is free of hidden bias, time to cover content during school hours, teachers capable of implementing content standards, adequate educational resources, respect for diversity, and ancillary services to meet the mental and social welfare needs of all students. Research indicates that developmentally appropriate instruction is not just a function of age or grade; rather, it depends on students' prior opportunities to learn. OTL also refers to the absence of barriers that prevent learning. Today, NCLB includes OTL in its accountability structure for schools and teachers as a vehicle for improved student achievement.

Learning is an active process that allows students the opportunity to construct understanding through empirical investigation and group interaction. OTL is facilitated through classrooms that focus on higher-order thinking skills, problem solving, substantive conversation, and real-world contexts. Such classrooms engage students in social and interactive mathematical inquiry accomplished through evidence-based discussion and reflection on learning.

OTL is enhanced by linking students' learning to their social and cultural identity. The premise of culturally responsive curriculum and pedagogy is that students become more engaged in mathematical content when that content is significant to cultural beliefs and values. Using a context that students recognize and incorporating various role models amplifies their confidence and comfort with the content. These strategies demonstrate that everyone can succeed in mathematics.

Teachers' attitudes and expectations can affect student achievement by increasing or decreasing students' effort and performance. By varying instruction, understanding the differences in needs and learning styles of individual students, and fostering discourse, teachers facilitate the development of learning communities and create a climate that improves student achievement.

Implications to Think About

Skilled and qualified teachers, school counselors, administrators, and education policymakers can convey high expectations and help raise students' self-esteem and performance. Administrators and policymakers can ensure that teachers are prepared appropriately for all levels of instruction. For instance, high school administrators can provide teachers with adequate instructional time through appropriate class scheduling, and counselors who assign classes must see appropriate higher-level mathematics coursework as a goal for all students; graduation requirements should reflect the importance of algebra, geometry, and higher mathematics in students' future careers. Elementary school administrators should also emphasize the importance of allocating adequate daily instructional time for mathematics.

A standards-based curriculum combined with the creative use of classroom strategies can provide a learning environment that both honors the mathematical strengths of all learners and nurtures students in areas where they are most challenged. By including mathematics content from a variety of cultures and personal experiences, teachers enhance the learning experience for all students. When instruction is anchored in the context of each learner's world, students are more likely to take ownership for and determine the direction of their own learning. Teachers, armed with OTL strategies, help students take responsibility for their own level of achievement.

To foster good mathematics teaching and high student achievement, adequate resources for classroom instruction should be available to all students. For a rich variety of investigations, students should use mathematical and technological tools, such as manipulatives, calculators, and computers. Schools that support equal access to mathematics supplies, equipment, and instructional resources are more likely to produce a student population with higher mathematical literacy.

Resources for Learning More

Duschl, R. A., Schweingruber, H. A., & Shouse, A. W. (Eds.). (2007). *Taking science to school: Learning and teaching sciences in grades K–8.*

Geary, D. C., Boykin, A. W., Embreton, S., Reyna, V., Siegler, R., Berch, D. B., et al. (2008). "Report of the task group on learning processes."

Herman, J. L., & Abedi, J. (2004). *Issues in assessing English language learners' opportunity to learn mathematics.*

Kilpatrick, J., & Swafford, J. (Eds.). (2002). *Helping children learn mathematics.*

Lester, F. K. (Ed.). (2007). *Second handbook of research on mathematics teaching and learning.*

Marzano, R. J. (2003). *What works in schools: Translating research into action.*

North Central Regional Educational Laboratory. (2004). *Connecting with the learner: An equity toolkit.*

Tomlinson, C. A. (2003). *Fulfilling the promise of the differentiated classroom: Strategies and tools for responsive teaching.*

1

How can teachers best address different learning styles?

Research and Ideas to Know About

Learning styles consist of personal characteristics, strengths, and preferences describing how individuals acquire, store, and process information. Learning-style factors include information-processing modes, environmental and instructional preferences, cognitive capabilities, and personality features. Individuals might demonstrate a balance among the dimensions of a learning style, or they might show strengths and weaknesses that affect course success and, eventually, career choice. Groups of students from different cultures might exhibit distinct predominant learning styles, though often such generalizations about learning styles and cultural background are not valid because of broad intragroup variations.

Learning styles not only influence how individuals learn, but also how they teach. Teachers often instruct in the same manner in which they were taught, even if the teaching style does not support the learning style that most students prefer. Teachers who are aware of their own teaching styles are able to make better choices of instructional strategies that promote student learning. They can interpret students' questions, comments, and answers in the context of learning-style variations.

Students need to know their own learning-style strengths and weaknesses and to develop a set of learning strategies that allows them to use their strengths and compensate for their weaknesses. When students receive instruction in the use of various learning strategies, they become more efficient and effective in studying and more likely to attribute success or failure to their choices rather than to their innate ability. Teachers who have taught their students about learning styles find that students learn the material better because they are more aware of their thinking processes. Students who are conscious of learning-style differences develop interpersonal communication skills critical to adult success. Some findings from longitudinal studies suggest that students who are aware of learning-style differences can better apply knowledge, are more satisfied with instruction, and have enhanced self-confidence.

When teaching and learning styles are significantly mismatched, students can be inattentive, bored, or discouraged and often perform poorly.

Implications to Think About

Learning-style strengths and weaknesses can influence task success and overall achievement. It is important to remember that learning styles are *preferences*, not traits or abilities. Available tools for assessing learning (and teaching) styles can provide *clues*, not labels, to personal styles. Students should know their personal learning strengths and be able to use that knowledge to improve on weaknesses. Students also need to learn strategies for coping with varied learning environments as well as how to modify or generalize strategies for novel situations. Strategy use includes knowledge about the strategy, when to use it, and how to tell if it worked.

When teaching and learning styles are significantly mismatched, students can be inattentive, bored, or discouraged and often perform poorly. In response, teachers may become overly critical, misinterpret poor scores as low ability (which exacerbates the situation), or become discouraged with teaching. Therefore, teachers must know how to identify learning and teaching styles and how to teach students to use various learning strategies. Teachers can use differentiated instruction that is varied enough to meet students' needs while respecting diversity. Diverse learners benefit from choices among standards-based learning methods, tasks, products, and assessments.

If instructors teach exclusively in a student's less preferred style, the student's discomfort can interfere with learning. However, students benefit from experience with nonpreferred learning styles. Preferred styles are not static, and skill development in nonpreferred modes encourages mental dexterity. Using a new learning style in the early stages of a unit may be more efficient than introducing a new learning style later in the unit. Teachers must balance instructional methods so that all students receive some instruction in their preferred styles but also have opportunities to practice learning in less preferred modes. Teachers who vary their methods will be more effective than those who limit their instruction to one or two methods.

In assessing students whose learning will be demonstrated through different learning styles, a teacher should consider the criteria for success. Students may demonstrate learning in various ways, depending on learning styles, but in a standards-based classroom, the standards make the expectations for learning clear.

Resources for Learning More

Armstrong, T. (1994). *Multiple intelligences in the classroom.*

Burke, K., & Dunn, R. (2002, Spring). "Teaching math effectively to elementary students."

Felder, R. (1996, December). "Matters of style."

Gardner, H. (1993). *Multiple intelligences: The theory in practice.*

McKeachie, W. J. (1995, November). "Learning styles can become learning strategies."

Oberer, J. J. (2003, Spring). "Effects of learning-style teaching on elementary students' behaviors, achievement, and attitudes."

Silver, H. F., Strong, R. W., & Perini, M. J. (2000). *So each may learn: Integrating learning styles and multiple intelligences.*

Spoon, J. C., & Schell, J. W. (1998, Winter). "Aligning student learning styles with instructor teaching styles."

Sprenger, M. (2003). *Differentiation through learning styles and memory.*

1

How can mathematics teachers support English language learners?

Research and Ideas to Know About

English language learners make up one of the fastest growing groups among the school-aged population in the United States. Since the early 1990s, this population has grown 169 percent in comparison to the general school population, which has grown only 12 percent. According to the National Clearinghouse for English Language Acquisition (NCELA), in 2005–2006, the ELL student population stood at more than 5 million. Although collectively they speak more than four hundred different languages, approximately 79 percent of ELLs in the United States are from Spanish-language backgrounds. By 2015, nearly 30 percent of the U.S. school-aged population could be ELLs.

This growth presents unique challenges to teachers in reform-oriented mathematics classrooms rich in problem solving, reasoning, and communication. In such classrooms, ELLs are expected to "talk math," which requires the use of precise and unambiguous academic language to express mathematical knowledge. This language requirement can become a barrier to ELLs' understanding.

It is a common misconception that mathematics is a "universal language," in which the use of numbers and symbols are culture free. ELLs who are native Chinese or Arabic speakers, for example, might not know the Latin alphabet and must become familiar with these letters not only in the written language, but also as symbols in algebraic and other mathematical representations. Academic language is central to the learning of mathematics, yet learners are not explicitly taught to read, write, or speak mathematically. In many mathematics classrooms and curricula, language demands go unnoticed and unattended to. This presents particular difficulties for ELLs; although they generally acquire social language in two years, the acquisition of academic language and literacy skills needed in the mathematics classroom can take seven to twelve years.

ELLs need specific support to understand and solve the word problems used for mathematics assessment and instruction. Challenging terms for ELLs commonly found in these problems include words that express quantitative relationships (such as *scarcely, next, less*, and *younger*) and words that link phrases and sentences and express a logical relationship (such as *if, alike, opposite of, not quite*, and *whether*).

Students who speak a first language other than English should not face special barriers to learning mathematics. Expanded opportunities to develop mathematical understanding and proficiency should be offered to ELL students who need them.

In 2005–2006, the ELL student population stood at more than 5 million. Although collectively they speak more than four hundred different languages, approximately 79 percent of ELLs in the United States are from Spanish-language backgrounds.

Implications to Think About

ELLs present a unique set of challenges to teachers because of the central role academic language plays in the acquisition and assessment of mathematics. Many ELLs have good conversational English skills; however, many lack the academic language that is central to success with academic texts and school in general. This lack of proficiency with academic language affects their ability to comprehend and analyze texts (especially at the middle and high school levels) and limits their ability to write and express themselves effectively in mathematics.

When planning lessons, teachers with ELLs in the mathematics classroom should take the following guidance into consideration:

- Identify language objectives alongside content objectives in daily lesson plans.

- Incorporate instructional support for oral and written language as it relates to mathematical content.

- Provide varied and frequent opportunities for students to reflect on and use mathematics vocabulary, both orally and in writing.

- Plan structured discussions that give students the chance to explain their thinking and reasoning orally, such as in think-alouds.

- Supplement instruction with real objects, math manipulatives, visuals, body language, facial expressions, gestures, and hands-on experiences.

- Link new information to students' background knowledge by giving hints about what they are going to experience.

- Provide, model, and practice cooperative learning opportunities so that students can hear and use the language of mathematics while simultaneously developing their own mathematical understanding.

- Adapt homework to meet the individual students' stage of language acquisition.

Because the problem-solving process varies in other countries, teachers must use their mathematical background to understand the range of algorithms that students might use. Teachers of English to Speakers of Other Languages has developed English Language Proficiency Standards for preK–12 that provide specific recommendations for developing an ELL's oral language and literacy through mathematics content.

Resources for Learning More

Brown, C. L., Cady, J. A., & Taylor, P. M. (2009, May). "Problem solving and the English language learner."

Francis, D. J., Rivera, M., Lesaux, N., Kieffer, M., & Rivera, H. (2006). *Practical guidelines for the education of English language learners: Research-based recommendations for instruction and academic interventions.*

Hill, J. D., & Flynn, K. M. (2006). *Classroom instruction that works with English language learners.*

National Clearinghouse for English Language Acquisition. (2009). *Frequently asked questions.*

National Council of Teachers of Mathematics. (2008b, September). *Teaching mathematics to English language learners: A position of the National Council of Teachers of Mathematics.*

Perkins, I., & Flores, A. (2002, February). "Mathematical notations and procedures of recent immigrant students."

Schleppegrell, M. J. (2007, April). "The linguistic challenges of mathematics teaching and learning: A research review."

Slavit, D., & Ernst-Slavit, G. (2007, November). "Teaching mathematics and English to English language learners simultaneously."

Teachers of English to Speakers of Other Languages. (2006). *PreK–12 English language proficiency standards.*

Teachers of English to Speakers of Other Languages. (2007). *Teachers of English to speakers of other languages.*

Winsor, M. S. (2007, December). "Bridging the language barrier in mathematics."

1

What instructional strategies help students with disabilities?

Research and Ideas to Know About

The Individuals with Disabilities Education Act of 1997 (IDEA) mandates that students with disabilities have access to the general education curriculum. This legislation has resulted in an increased number of students with disabilities in regular education classrooms taught by teachers who have become overwhelmed by the challenges of responding to the needs of all of their students.

Teachers have found that just having a list of accommodations and strategies for working with this student population is not enough.

Teachers have found that just having a list of accommodations and strategies for working with this student population is not enough. To be effective, the strategies have to be connected to the mathematics curricula, to the specific needs of individual students, and to the particular classroom setting. To determine how to frame learning to meet the needs of their learners, teachers must first understand the areas in which students' strengths and weaknesses affect mathematical learning.

The Education Development Center's Addressing Accessibility in Mathematics project has identified six areas that play an important role in students' abilities to access mathematics: conceptual processing, language, visual-spatial processing, organization, memory, and attention.

1   Problems with *conceptual processing* are often seen when students have difficulty remembering the meaning of symbols, making generalizations, visualizing and identifying patterns, and making connections between new problems and those previously solved.

2   *Language* problems vary from difficulty decoding words and comprehending text to having difficulty with the auditory processing of verbal information.

3   *Visual-spatial processing* problems are often manifested in the mathematics classroom when students have difficulty representing concepts visually (such as on graphs or 3-D models), are distracted by crowded pages of text, or cannot read standard-sized text.

4   Complex problems make many organizational demands on students. Students who struggle with *organization* have a hard time starting problems, get confused by multiple steps in making tables and graphs, and tend to need help breaking a large task into steps.

5   *Memory* problems often are evidenced when students have difficulty retrieving information accurately or efficiently, even though they might have successfully stored the knowledge at a previous time. Students with memory problems struggle with multistep tasks (such as long division or solving algebraic equations), as they often confuse or omit crucial steps.

6   Students with *attention* problems sometimes miss important information when it is presented in class or overlook it when it appears in a problem. Attention problems can affect procedural knowledge when students miss an important step in a procedure and can also affect problem solving that requires students to use part of a situation to develop a hypothesis.

Implications to Think About

Many teachers enter classrooms unprepared to work with children who have special needs. Mathematics textbooks often have poorly integrated effective instructional practices for students with special needs, leaving teachers with little or no direction on how to meet their students' needs. Some students might need strategies to help them understand the mathematics, whereas others might need help carrying out tasks in the lesson.

Traditionally, students with disabilities received direct instruction on how to perform an algorithm using procedural steps without being provided an opportunity to develop a conceptual understanding of the procedure. When planning lessons, teachers need to incorporate instructional strategies that will increase the students' ability to access both the procedural and conceptual mathematical content being taught. These strategies may include:

- Helping students understand tasks

- Providing multiple ways for students to access mathematics

- Building student independence

- Promoting understanding through mathematical discourse (written and oral)

- Helping students manage tasks and organization

- Adjusting tasks to student needs

- Modeling, providing, and consistently implementing a structured note-taking process (such as two-column notes or Cornell notes)

- Using multisensory techniques to model problem-solving strategies

- Ensuring that the sequence of instruction moves from the concrete to the representational to the abstract

- Providing multiple opportunities for students to practice and acquire fundamental skills and understandings

Teachers can build accessibility into their classroom environments by using strategic seating plans, organizational systems, and word walls, and by reducing visual and auditory distractions. When students work with physical manipulatives, teachers must understand that the act of physically manipulating multiple pieces may create such a high cognitive load on students' thinking processes that they could lose sight of the mathematical concept being taught.

To make mathematics more accessible to students with disabilities, teachers need opportunities to plan proactively and to expand their own repertoires of strategies. The challenge of reaching a wide range of students becomes less overwhelming when teachers share their perspectives and build on one another's expertise. Collaboration with special education teachers helps mathematics teachers expand their thinking about students' abilities and needs as they relate to learning mathematics.

Resources for Learning More

Allsopp, D., Lovin, L., Green, G., & Savage-Davis, E. (2003, February). "Why students with special needs have difficulty learning mathematics and what teachers can do to help."

Brodesky, A. R., Gross, F. E., McTigue, A. S., & Tierney, C. C. (2004, October). "Planning strategies for students with special needs: A professional development activity."

Education Development Center. (2005). The K–12 mathematics curriculum center.

Education Development Center. (2007). Addressing accessibility in mathematics.

Individuals with Disabilities Education Act Amendments of 1997. (1997).

Jayanthi, M., Gersten, R., & Baker, S. (2008). Mathematics instruction for students with learning disabilities or difficulty learning mathematics: A guide for teachers.

Kilpatrick, J., Swafford, J., & Findell, B. (Eds.). (2001). Adding it up: Helping children learn mathematics.

Maccini, P., & Gagnon, J. C. (2000, January). "Best practices for teaching mathematics to secondary students with special needs."

Maccini, P., Mulcahy, C. A., & Wilson, M. G. (2007, February). "A follow-up of mathematics interventions for secondary students with learning disabilities."

National Council of Supervisors of Mathematics. (2008c, Winter). Improving student achievement in mathematics for students with special needs.

How does response to intervention impact mathematics teaching?

Research and Ideas to Know About

Response to intervention (RTI) is an approach to intervention that generates data to inform instruction and identify students who may need special education or other related services. Although the term *RTI* is relatively new, the approach is similar to various initiatives implemented since the early 1990s; these prior initiatives focused on collaborative problem-solving approaches to provide interventions for struggling general education students. With the 2004 reauthorization of the Individuals with Disabilities Education Act, states and school districts began considering RTI as an identification method for learning disabilities.

In the RTI model, primary prevention takes place in the general education classroom and is used to examine students' unresponsiveness to otherwise effective education. RTI provides faithfully implemented research-based curricula and intensive interventions in a general education setting as a way to distinguish between students who perform poorly due to instructional factors and those with learning disabilities who need more intensive and specialized instruction.

RTI focuses on early intervention through a multitiered approach in which each tier provides increasingly intensive instruction. Regardless of the number of tiers, all systems share the same goals. A strong multitiered RTI model requires the use of evidence-based practices, regular screening, preventative methods, progress monitoring, and diagnostic tests. RTI is typically thought of as having three tiers:

1 The instruction that all students in a classroom receive

2 Additional assistance for students who demonstrate difficulties on the universal screening methods or who demonstrate weak progress

3 Intensive interventions for students who are not benefiting from Tier 2; in some cases, special education services are included in Tier 3

> RTI focuses on early intervention through a multitiered approach in which each tier provides increasingly intensive instruction.

Implications to Think About

In literacy, the RTI model is backed by a strong body of research; in mathematics, however, this body of research is just beginning to emerge. In April 2009, the Institute of Education Sciences (IES) tasked a panel with reviewing the current research on RTI in mathematics and compiling a list of recommendations for assisting elementary and middle school students who are struggling in mathematics. The eight resulting recommendations were published in the IES practice guide by Gersten and colleagues, *Assisting Students Struggling With Mathematics: Response to Intervention (RtI) for Elementary and Middle Schools*:

1 All students should be screened to identify those at risk for potential mathematics difficulties and provide interventions to those identified as at risk.

2 Instructional materials for students receiving interventions should focus intensely on in-depth treatment of whole numbers in kindergarten through grade 5 and on rational numbers in grades 4 through 8. These materials should be selected by committee.

3 Instruction during the intervention should be explicit and systematic. This includes providing models of proficient problem solving, verbalization of thought processes, guided practice, corrective feedback, and frequent cumulative review.

4 Interventions should include instruction on solving word problems that is based on common underlying structures.

5 Intervention materials should include opportunities for students to work with visual representations of mathematical ideas, and interventionists should be proficient in using visual representations of mathematical ideas.

6 Interventions at all grade levels should devote about ten minutes in each session to building fluent retrieval of basic arithmetic facts.

7 The progress of students receiving supplemental instruction as well as other students who are at risk should be monitored.

8 Motivational strategies should be included in tier 2 and tier 3 interventions. (2009, p. 6)

At the heart of the RTI model is personalized instruction, during which each student's unique needs are evaluated and appropriate instruction is provided, so that all students will succeed. Even with the small amount of research on RTI in mathematics, some already-observed advantages are increased accountability for all learners as a result of the focus on student outcomes, more students receiving early intervention, and increased collaboration and shared responsibility among all stakeholders (special educators, classroom teachers, parents, teachers of ELLs).

Resources for Learning More

Brown, J. E., & Doolittle, J. (2008). *A cultural, linguistic, and ecological framework for response to intervention with English language learners.*

Bryant, B. R., & Pedrotty Bryant, D. (2008, Winter). "Introduction to the special series: Mathematics and learning disabilities."

Gersten, R., Beckmann, S., Clarke, B., Foegen, A., Marsh, L., Star, J. R., et al. (2009). *Assisting students struggling with mathematics: Response to intervention (RtI) for elementary and middle schools.*

National Joint Committee on Learning Disabilities. (2005, June). *Responsiveness to intervention and learning disabilities.*

Newman-Gonchar, R., Clarke, B., & Gersten, R. (2009). *A summary of nine key studies: Multitier intervention and response to interventions for students struggling in mathematics.*

VanDerHeyden, A. (n.d.). *RTI and math instruction.*

CHAPTER 2

Teaching Mathematics

Learning and teaching mathematics are complex, active processes. Teachers constantly make decisions as they facilitate an environment in which students are active learners. They also must undertake long-term planning to connect daily efforts to the broader education of each student. At the same time, teachers share responsibility for their students' successes with other parts of the educational community, including their colleagues, their institutions, and the policies of the educational system.

The NCTM's *Principles and Standards for School Mathematics* outlines theoretical and practical knowledge and understandings about mathematics, how children acquire mathematics content, and mathematics teaching techniques that facilitate each child's learning. Effective professional development moves teachers toward the goals spelled out in these professional standards for teaching mathematics. Because a teacher's classroom decisions affect each student's achievement, teachers need to avail themselves of strategies as varied as their students' educational needs.

What instructional methods support mathematical reasoning and problem solving?

Research and Ideas to Know About

Research on best instructional methods for teaching and learning mathematical reasoning and problem solving consistently and clearly identifies the need for teachers to provide mathematically rich environments conducive to investigations.

Effective mathematics instruction occurs in community settings in which teachers carefully select problems, materials, and grouping practices; provide opportunity for mathematics discourse; and use assessment practices designed to provoke and support student thinking. Mathematics instruction must connect with, build on, and refine the understandings, intuitions, and resourcefulness that students bring to the classroom. Building students' mathematical reasoning and problem-solving skills requires teachers to teach mathematics as the power of thought rather than the power of discrete facts.

Instructional methods that support and promote student sharing, questioning, and active listening enhance student reasoning and problem-solving skills. Instructional practice should promote explorations that are supported by easy access to a wide variety of tools designed to accomplish a task. The tools students use influence the kinds of understanding they develop.

Both mathematics and science have standards of proof: an argument must be supported by evidence, and conclusions must be logically derived. Through questions and clarifications, teachers follow the evolution of student thinking in order to guide it effectively, and at appropriate times—not prematurely—they introduce current ideas. Teachers who orchestrate the integration of conceptual, procedural, and factual knowledge provide the "sense making" that students need in order to develop confidence in their ability to reason and solve problems.

> Building students' mathematical reasoning and problem-solving skills requires teachers to teach mathematics as the power of thought rather than the power of discrete facts.

Implications to Think About

Classrooms that promote mathematical reasoning and problem solving typically are supportive, collegial communities. Teachers make instructional choices that support the opportunity for all children to learn important mathematics. Teachers find ways to support students as they work through challenging tasks without taking over the process of thinking for them, thus eliminating the challenge. Teachers promote mathematical discourse by focusing on whole-class discussions in which students engage in mathematical reasoning and debate and talk about mathematics in ways that reveal their understanding of concepts. Teachers encourage productive discourse by asking strategic questions about how a problem was solved and why a particular method was chosen. For productive discussions to take place, norms should be established that encourage students to listen and understand one anothers' explanations, ask questions, and feel comfortable explaining and justifying their own responses. An effective classroom model includes a structure in which teachers pose interesting, challenging problems or tasks to the class as a whole. Time is allotted for students to:

- Individually ponder appropriate strategies

- Identify tools to assist in solving the problem

- Work in small groups to explore and discuss ideas and solve the problem

- Report their findings to the class

Students are challenged to approach a problem by using reasoning, logic and powers of observation, models, evidence, examples, and counterexamples to discover meaningful patterns. Opportunities are provided for students who solved a problem differently to share their procedures, thus encouraging diverse thinking. Through classroom interactions, students develop mathematical ideas and conjectures and learn to evaluate their own thinking and that of others.

Effective instructional methods that promote mathematical reasoning include:

- Comparing and clarifying

- Analyzing information that leads to summarizing

- Creating graphic representations, such as pictures and pictographs

Tools or manipulatives are integral resources for building understanding, but effective teachers recognize that the tools themselves do not provide meaning. Rather, they help students make connections.

Resources for Learning More

Bransford, J. D., Brown, A. L., Cocking, R. R., Donovan, M. S., & Pellegrino, J. W. (Eds.). (2000). *How people learn: Brain, mind, experience, and school.*

Cawelti, G. (Ed.). (2004). *Handbook of research on improving student achievement.*

Fuson, K. C., Kalchman, M., & Bransford, J. D. (2005). "Mathematical understanding: An introduction."

Hiebert, J., Carpenter, T. P., Fennema, E., Fuson, K. C., Wearne, D., Murray, H., et al. (1997). *Making sense: Teaching and learning mathematics with understanding.*

Martin, T. S. (Ed.). (2007). *Mathematics teaching today: Improving practice, improving student learning.*

Marzano, R. J., Norford, J. S., Paynter, D. E., Pickering, D. J., & Gaddy, B. B. (2001). *A handbook for classroom instruction that works.*

Marzano, R. J., Pickering, D. J., & Pollock, J. E. (2001). *Classroom instruction that works: Research-based strategies for increasing student achievement.*

National Council of Teachers of Mathematics. (2000). *Principles and standards for school mathematics.*

Pashler, H., Bain, P. M., Bottge, B. A., Graesser, A., Koedinger, K., McDaniel, M., et al. (2007). *Organizing instruction and study to improve student learning: A practice guide.*

Thompson, C. L., & Zeuli, J. S. (1999). "The frame and the tapestry: Standards-based reform and professional development."

2

How is mathematical thinking addressed in the mathematics classroom?

Research and Ideas to Know About

Mathematical processes include problem solving, reasoning and proof, communication, connections, and representation. Mathematical thinking can help students acquire and use content knowledge and skills. At one time, the ability to solve mathematical problems was believed to be automatically derived from knowing the mathematics. We now know that for all mathematical processes, students need a well-organized understanding of the mathematics involved and experience solving a wide variety of problems. Simply put, students need many opportunities to use mathematical processes.

"Being able to reason is essential to understanding mathematics."

—National Council of Teachers of Mathematics, 2000, p. 56

Reasoning and proof are mathematical processes that relate closely to scientific inquiry. In the process of proof, mathematicians often start by testing a mathematical statement with random numbers; then they look at some special cases—such as negatives, fractions, or infinity—and test again. From this information they can formulate a hypothesis and try to deduce the final result. The process of proof is a formal procedure for expressing reasoning. Mathematical reasoning also includes graphic and algebraic reasoning, proportional and probabilistic reasoning, and geometrical and statistical reasoning.

Students amend and refine their ideas when communicating their understanding of mathematics. Communicating mathematics includes reading, writing, discourse, and using multiple representations. Definitions are important in mathematics, and students need to not only understand the role they play, but also use them in their mathematical work.

Explaining connections among mathematical ideas and teaching the different ways of representing a single mathematical idea will help students build deeper understandings. Similarly, showing the power and practicality of mathematics forges connections with other subject areas and the real world.

Representations of mathematical ideas can be visual—such as equations, graphs, pictures, and charts—or they can be in the mind of the student as he or she interprets the mathematical situation. Students' mental representations of problems affect how they go about solving them. Students can also use verbal descriptions and examples to communicate their ideas and findings. Students with a well-developed understanding of a concept can represent it in various ways.

Implications to Think About

Selecting worthwhile mathematical tasks that contain sound, significant mathematics is important. Tasks should be based on students' understandings, interests, and experiences and should capitalize on the range of ways that diverse students learn mathematics. Teachers should choose tasks that require students to engage in mathematical thinking and problem solving, draw out students' thinking through effective questioning, and encourage reflection and sense making.

When selecting tasks, teachers should ensure that the tasks meet the following criteria:

- They are authentic in that they come from the students' environment.

- They are challenging yet within the reach of students.

- They pique students' curiosity.

- They encourage students to make sense of mathematical ideas.

- They encourage multiple perspectives and interrelated mathematical ideas.

- They nest skill development in the context of problem solving.

- They promote communication about mathematics.

- They represent mathematics as an ongoing human activity.

- They promote the development of all students' dispositions to do mathematics.

Reasoning skills need to be continually developed through curricula that build on students' existing knowledge and also present ideas that require new knowledge and understanding.

Connecting mathematical ideas promotes understanding so that students can apply that knowledge to learn new topics and solve unfamiliar problems. Students develop understanding through the construction of relationships by extending and applying mathematical knowledge, reflecting about experiences, articulating what they know, and making mathematical knowledge pertinent to their own lives. All processes imply making connections.

Resources for Learning More

Driscoll, M. (1999). *Fostering algebraic thinking: A guide for teachers, grades 6–10.*

Driscoll, M. (with Wing DiMatteo, R., Nikula, J., & Egan, M.). (2007). *Fostering geometric thinking: A guide for teachers, grades 5–10.*

Fennema, E., & Romberg, T. A. (Eds.). (1999). *Mathematics classrooms that promote understanding.*

Hiebert, J., Carpenter, T. P., Fennema, E., Fuson, K. C., Wearne, D., Murray, H., et al. (1997). *Making sense: Teaching and learning mathematics with understanding.*

Hudson, P., & Miller, S. P. (2005). *Designing and implementing mathematics instruction for students with diverse learning needs.*

Martin, T. S. (Ed.). (2007). *Mathematics teaching today: Improving practice, improving student learning.*

Rigelman, N. R. (2007, February). "Fostering mathematical thinking and problem solving: The teacher's role."

Romberg, T. A., & Kaput, J. J. (1999). "Mathematics worth teaching, mathematics worth understanding."

2

What role does teacher questioning play in learning mathematics?

Research and Ideas to Know About

Teachers maximize learning when they encourage questions, expect students to elaborate on and explain their answers, and provide frequent feedback. In classrooms with effective instruction, large- and small-group discussions commonly occur between the teacher and students as well as among students.

Effective mathematics teachers—those who are highly rated by their students and whose students perform well on both content and problem-solving skills assessments—ask well-planned questions of all types. Compared to less effective teachers, they pose more questions with higher cognitive demand and ask more follow-up questions, and their students ask more questions as well. Effective teachers orchestrate productive discussions through purposefully prepared questions.

Students in high-performing and conceptually oriented classrooms are expected to share ideas with others. Striving to explain their thinking helps students clarify their ideas, even when their thinking is not totally clear or their understanding is not well formulated. Students who must explain their thinking organize their thoughts and analyze the strategies they used.

Studies of questioning in typical mathematics classrooms confirm that most questions make minimal demands on student thinking. Low-level questions—which include questions with yes/no answers; questions that require guessing or simple recall of fact, formula, or procedure; leading or rhetorical questions; and those answered immediately by the teacher—do not give a good picture of a student's grasp of a concept. Answers are often immediately judged right or wrong by the teacher, and discussion moves to the next question. Lengthening the wait time between posing a question and expecting an answer, however, increases the number of responses, student confidence, responses by less-able students, and reflective responses.

> Effective teachers orchestrate productive discussions through purposefully prepared questions.

Implications to Think About

Better questioning practices lead to better learning by all students. The foundation of good questioning is strong content knowledge, which is critical in enabling teachers to understand and respond to students' questions. Teachers must also have a firm understanding of how students learn, so they can anticipate students' misunderstandings and plan appropriate questions.

Good questioning requires skill and planning. Strategies to improve questioning techniques include the following:

- Plan questions while preparing lessons. Write out questions to launch a lesson as well as questions to use during exploration.

- Choose different questions for varied purposes—clarifying, redirecting, summarizing, extension, open-ended, and reflection.

- Occasionally tape lessons to monitor levels of questioning.

- Focus questions on searching for student understanding; deemphasize right or wrong answers.

- Ask students to paraphrase what's been said. This improves attentiveness and assesses comprehension.

- Listen carefully to student responses, and assume that every answer is meaningful and "correct" to that student. Answers give insight into the student's mind and illuminate misunderstandings. They provide an opportunity for the teacher to learn about each student.

- Begin lessons with rich questions or problems to engage students and lead to new understanding of important content. Provide a variety of tools to assist mathematical exploration.

- Intentionally provide multiple opportunities for discussion and social interaction around mathematics ideas, thereby creating an environment conducive to high-quality mathematical discourse.

- Allocate time carefully. Make notes from class to class on effective amounts of time for each explanation.

- Increase wait time. An observant teaching partner can assist.

- Model self-questioning by "acting out" your thinking when you approach a problem. "I wonder what I should do next. Maybe I should try . . ."

Resources for Learning More

Cawelti, G. (Ed.). (2004). *Handbook of research on improving student achievement.*

Chapin, S. H. (2003). *Classroom discussions: Using math talk to help students learn, grades 1–6.*

Hiebert, J., Carpenter, T. P., Fennema, E., Fuson, K. C., Wearne, D., Murray, H., et al. (1997). *Making sense: Teaching and learning mathematics with understanding.*

Johnson, J. (2000). *Teaching and learning mathematics: Using research to shift from the "yesterday" mind to the "tomorrow" mind.*

Kilpatrick, J., Martin, W. G., & Schifter, D. (Eds.). (2003). *A research companion to principles and standards for school mathematics.*

Martin, T. S. (Ed.). (2007). *Mathematics teaching today: Improving practice, improving student learning.*

PBS TeacherLine. (2006). *Developing mathematical thinking with effective questions.*

Sullivan, P., & Lilburn, P. (2002). *Good questions for math teaching: Why ask them and what to ask, K–6.*

Walsh, J. A., & Sattes, B. D. (2005). *Quality questioning: Research-based practices to engage every learner.*

2

How can teachers motivate students to enjoy and want to learn mathematics?

Research and Ideas to Know About

Students' perceptions of their performance in mathematics influence their motivation to learn. Student effort depends on expectations of success, whether the task is considered to be of value, and whether the task was presented in an engaging way. The task must be challenging enough to compel attention but also must offer a high likelihood of success given appropriate effort.

Teachers should encourage students to attribute their successes to diligence and perseverance, and their lack of success to insufficient effort, confusion, or poor choice of strategy—not to lack of ability. Students will feel more capable in mathematics if they attribute their success to effort and feel their success is meaningful, than if they attribute success to ability, luck, or external influences.

The classroom environment is important. Teachers' attitudes and actions greatly influence student motivation toward learning mathematics. Successful teachers are more knowledgeable about mathematics and are committed to the success of all students. Students need to engage in classroom discourse in which they respectfully listen to, respond to, and question different ways of thinking. Students also need to learn to make conjectures, evaluate approaches and tools, analyze strategies, and present convincing arguments. An environment that allows for conceptual exploration and has space and tools for investigation helps students make sense of mathematics both independently and collaboratively.

Intrinsic motivation generally yields greater success than extrinsic incentives. Activities that build a rich understanding of mathematics increase intrinsic motivation; for many students, nothing is as exciting as learning. If students value mathematics, they become more skillful, achieve at higher levels, are more persistent problem solvers, and exhibit greater confidence. Extrinsic motivations such as grades and social pressure, when tied to student values, can also have positive effects. *Foundations for Success*, the final report of the National Mathematics Advisory Panel, stresses the importance of effort on improved student performance in mathematics and encourages all educators to help both students and parents understand the effect of effort on learning.

Interesting contexts stimulate learning and retention. Cooperative group interactions and social construction of knowledge contribute positively to student engagement and attainment. Multiple approaches allow students of different learning dispositions to gain access to problems, thus increasing motivation.

> Students will feel more capable in mathematics if they attribute success to their effort and feel their success is meaningful.

Implications to Think About

Teachers awaken the joy of learning by creating a climate of choice, freedom from judgment, belief in each student's abilities, and knowledge that talent is expressed in many ways. Students need opportunities to satisfy their curiosities, test their imaginations, create, wonder, and invent. Classrooms that encourage playfulness, vitality, sensitivity, humor, and joy are inviting and stimulating. Environments that allow students to approach mathematics in many ways—including manipulatives, technological tools, and hands-on activities—engage students' multiple intelligences.

Challenge and feedback are important factors in maximizing brain growth. When students are challenged too much or too little, they give up or become bored. Many environmental factors can provide challenge—time, materials, access, expectations, support, novelty, and even décor. Teachers can create intellectual challenge through problem solving, critical thinking, relevant projects, and complex activities.

Opportunities to reflect allow learners to provide their own feedback. While teacher feedback certainly motivates students to do better work, peer feedback that shows value and care allows students to assess their ideas and behaviors and makes learning more enjoyable. Feedback is most effective when it is specific, immediate, and gives the receiver explanation and a choice.

Our bodies use emotion and attention to survive and face challenges. We continually assess our internal and external environments to determine what's important. Emotion provides a quick, general assessment of the situation, whereas attention brings focus to the things that seem important. To help students thrive in an education environment, pedagogical considerations should include:

- Acceptance of and control over our emotions (beliefs regarding mathematics)

- Use of activities that provide emotional context (more easily recalled and remembered)

- Avoidance of emotional stress (self-esteem and mathematical confidence)

- Recognition of the relationship between emotions and health (an exciting atmosphere)

- Use of metacognitive activities (talking about why a particular mathematical method was pursued)

- Use of activities that promote social interaction (mathematics as a language)

Resources for Learning More

Armstrong, T. (1998). *Awakening genius in the classroom.*

Jensen, E. (1998). *Teaching with the brain in mind.*

Martin, T. S. (Ed.). (2007). *Mathematics teaching today: Improving practice, improving student learning.*

Marzano, R. J., Pickering, D. J., & Pollock, J. E. (2001). *Classroom instruction that works: Research-based strategies for increasing student achievement.*

Middleton, J. A., & Spanias, P. A. (1999, January). "Motivation for achievement in mathematics: Findings, generalizations, and criticisms of the recent research."

National Mathematics Advisory Panel. (2008). *Foundations for success: The final report of the National Mathematics Advisory Panel.*

Sprenger, M. (1999). *Learning and memory: The brain in action.*

Sylwester, R. (1995). *A celebration of neurons: An educator's guide to the human brain.*

2

What instructional strategies make mathematics more challenging and interesting to students?

Research and Ideas to Know About

The best instructional strategies respect the diversity of learners and use this diversity to enhance learning and achieve improved results. The American Psychological Association has developed fourteen research-based principles that focus primarily on learners' internal psychological factors but also acknowledge the interaction of external environmental factors with internal factors.

"Almost all, who have ever fully understood arithmetic, have been obliged to learn it over again in their own way."

—Warren Colburn, educator and mathematician

Following are six of the fourteen principles most relevant to this topic:

1   Learners link new information with existing knowledge.

2   Learners use metacognition to select and monitor mental processes.

3   Teachers can influence motivation and effort toward learning.

4   Learning is most effective when it matches developmental readiness, specifically as it relates to prior experiences and learning opportunities, rather than to age, grade, or maturity level.

5   Learning is a social activity.

6   Learning is more effective when instruction takes diversity into account.

Effective teachers know their students well—their strengths and weaknesses, their interests and preferences—and plan instruction to challenge all learners to meet high standards. To do this, teachers must find ways to surface students' prior mathematics knowledge and understandings so that knowledge gaps can be addressed, inconsistencies resolved, and understandings deepened.

Teachers must also learn about their students' backgrounds outside of school, so that mathematics instruction can be contextualized. They must include development of metacognitive strategies as well as social and communication skills in their classroom goals. Effective teachers understand what students know and need to learn and then challenge and support them to learn it well. Research has shown that instructional strategies that promote cooperation over competition allow students to use their cultural background to their advantage.

Implications to Think About

One way students learn is by connecting new ideas to prior knowledge. Teachers must help students come to view mathematics not as an isolated set of rules to memorize, but as the connection of ideas, mathematical domains, and concepts. Effective instruction combines guided questioning with lessons that build on the experiences and level of understanding that students already have. Selected strategies for accessing students' prior knowledge include the following:

- K-W-L (What do you know? What do you want to know? What did you learn?)

- Pretests

- Cueing and questioning

- Graphic organizers

- Think-alouds

- Quick writes

- Journal writing

Students benefit from time to reflect and gain a deeper understanding of mathematics as well as time to apply learned concepts and skills. As students struggle to solve problems, the teacher's role becomes one of active listening, clarifying issues, and probing student thinking. When incorporating an inquiry approach to mathematical problem solving, questions teachers might ask include the following:

- *What would happen if . . . ?*

- *Can you solve it another way?*

- *What are you thinking?*

- *Can you tell me more about that?*

- *Why do you think that will work?*

- *Can you think of a counterexample?*

Effective instructional strategies engage students in interesting situations and meaningful problems that emphasize making sense of mathematical ideas. Teachers should engage students in investigating a mathematical concept by posing an interesting and challenging problem that contains meaningful mathematical ideas and multiple potential pathways for reaching a solution. Students should use a variety of tools, including manipulative materials, calculators, web-based resources, and interactive electronic devices to explore mathematical concepts and make sense of them. At times, they should work on problems collaboratively so they can share their strategies. Lastly, students should explain their mathematical reasoning both orally and in writing, and have opportunities to write their own problems.

Resources for Learning More

American Psychological Association. (1997). *Learner-centered psychological principles.*

Colburn, W. (2009). *Colburn's first lessons: Intellectual arithmetic, upon the inductive method of instruction.*

Dowker, A. (1992, January). "Computational estimation strategies of professional mathematicians."

Flores, A. (2007, November). "Examining disparities in mathematics education: Achievement gap or opportunity gap?"

Heuser, D. (2000, January). "Mathematics workshop: Mathematics class becomes learner centered."

Ma, L. (1999). *Knowing and teaching elementary mathematics: Teachers' understanding of fundamental mathematics in China and the United States.*

Marzano, R. J., Norford, J. S., Paynter, D. E., Pickering, D. J., & Gaddy, B. B. (2001). *A handbook for classroom instruction that works.*

Marzano, R. J., Pickering, D. J., & Pollock, J. E. (2001). *Classroom instruction that works: Research-based strategies for increasing student achievement.*

National Mathematics Advisory Panel. (2008). *Foundations for success: The final report of the National Mathematics Advisory Panel.*

Reys, B. J., & Long, V. M. (1995, January). "Implementing the professional standards for teaching mathematics: Teacher as architect of mathematical tasks."

2

What role does vocabulary instruction play in the mathematics classroom?

Research and Ideas to Know About

To succeed academically, all students must develop an academic language distinct from their conversational language. Proficient use of this academic language is the key to content area learning. Evidence suggests that the single most important determinant of academic access for individual students is the mastery of this academic language. Even though factors such as motivation and persistence play important roles in the learning process, overstating the importance of academic language is not possible. To learn academic language, students must become familiar with academic vocabulary.

Learning academic vocabulary is more than looking up words in a dictionary or reading them in text. In fact, research indicates that wide reading is not sufficient in itself to ensure that students develop the necessary academic vocabulary to do well in school. The ultimate goal of learning vocabulary is to have students store meanings in their long-term memory and then to apply this memory as they construct meaning and comprehend text.

Specialized vocabulary terms broadly associated with mathematics (such as *number*, *angle*, and *equation*) and technical vocabulary terms associated with specific mathematical topics (such as *perfect numbers*, *quadratic equations*, *cosine*, and *mode*) must be directly taught. Research analysis shows that direct vocabulary instruction has an impressive track record of improving students' comprehension of academic content. In fact, student achievement increases by 33 percentile points when vocabulary instruction focuses on words important to the content the student is learning.

To increase student background knowledge and ability to comprehend academic content, Marzano suggests eight research-based characteristics of effective direct vocabulary instruction:

1   Effective vocabulary instruction does not rely on definitions.

2   Students must represent their knowledge of works in linguistic and nonlinguistic ways.

3   Effective vocabulary instruction involves the gradual shaping of word meanings through multiple exposures.

4   Teaching word parts enhances students' understanding of terms.

5   Different types of words require different types of instruction.

6   Students should discuss the terms they are learning.

7   Students should play with words.

8   Instruction should focus on terms that have a high probability of success. (2004, pp. 70–88)

> Learning academic vocabulary is more than looking up words in a dictionary or reading them in text.

Implications to Think About

Marzano, Pickering, and Pollock outline five steps for direct vocabulary instruction that provide a framework for making the task of learning vocabulary easier.

1 Present students with a brief explanation or description of the new term or phrase.

2 Present students with a nonlinguistic representation of the new term or phrase.

3 Ask students to generate their own explanation or description of the term or phrase.

4 Ask students to create their own nonlinguistic representation of the term or phrase.

5 Periodically ask students to review the accuracy of their explanations and representation. (2001, pp. 128–129)

When providing direct instruction to students on mathematical vocabulary, highlighting the terms with multiple meanings is important. For example, the word *table* can refer to a "times table" for multiplication facts or a "table of values" for graphing functions. However, *table* also has very different meanings and uses in nonmathematical contexts: a "timetable" for the bus route, the "table" you sit at to eat dinner, a "table of contents" in language arts, and the "periodic table" in chemistry. During vocabulary instruction, teachers must expose students to new words multiple times so that they can learn the word's meaning and pronunciation, as well as how its meaning may change in different contexts.

One of the best ways to learn a new word is to associate an image with the word. However, teachers should be cautious about overuse of one instructional strategy; they need to teach and model multiple strategies (such as the Frayer model, descriptive pattern, concept definition map, and word squares).

Direct vocabulary instruction is especially important when working with ELLs. One way to teach ELLs mathematical terms that has been promoted for many years is the use of cognates. Language *cognates* are words that have a common origin, making the connections between English and an ELL's native language easier to understand. Examples of cognates in mathematics include sum/*sumar*, addition/*adicion*, circumference/*circunferencia*, and cube/*cubo*.

Resources for Learning More

Adams, T. L., Thangata, F., & King, C. (2005, May). "'Weigh' to go! Exploring mathematical language."

Fischer, J., & Perez, R., Jr. (2008). *Understanding English through mathematics: A research based ELL approach to teaching all students.*

Marzano, R. J. (2004). *Building background knowledge for academic achievement: Research on what works in schools.*

Marzano, R. J., Pickering, D. J., & Pollock, J. E. (2001). *Classroom instruction that works: Research-based strategies for increasing student achievement.*

Paynter, D. E., Bodrova, E., & Doty, J. K. (2005). *For the love of words: Vocabulary instruction that works, grades K–6.*

Rubenstein, R. N. (2007, November). "Focused strategies for middle-grades mathematics vocabulary development."

Stone, B., & Urquhart, V. (2008). *Remove limits to learning with systematic vocabulary instruction.*

2

How does linking instruction and classroom assessment impact student learning?

Research and Ideas to Know About

Ongoing, embedded classroom assessment promotes student learning.

Classroom assessment, an essential tool for supporting and monitoring student progress toward mathematics standards, should be aligned with instruction. *Formative classroom assessment*, sometimes referred to as *assessment for learning*, is a systematic process of continuously gathering evidence about student learning. Interest in this type of assessment is growing. Teachers use the information they gather to adapt instruction to meet student needs as learning occurs. Linking instruction and classroom assessment has at least three notable benefits.

First, classroom assessment embedded within a unit reveals to teachers what individuals and groups of students know, understand, and can do with the material they are learning. Embedded assessment may include informal measures such as observation, student interviews, and exit tickets or more formal measures such as quizzes.

Second, ongoing, embedded classroom assessment promotes student learning. Classroom assessment should be accessible to students—that is, it asks them to use the skills and knowledge already mastered—and should contain valuable mathematics content. Students whose teachers use open-ended assessment items not only have improved attitudes toward mathematics, but also perform better on open-ended high-stakes assessment items than students whose teachers do not use them. According to the final report of the National Mathematics Advisory Panel, when teachers gather formative data and understand how to use the data to differentiate instruction, the effect on student learning can be significant.

Third, classroom assessment can help students monitor their own learning. When students know what is expected of them through rubrics, feedback, and grading criteria, they are better able to keep track of their own mastery of the material. When students know the scoring criteria by which a skill or concept will be assessed (such as written communication of their problem-solving strategy), they are more likely to meet those criteria.

One research study showed that teachers who used open-ended, embedded assessments discovered the limitations in their own understanding of mathematical concepts. Another study found that teachers who learned to incorporate open-ended assessment into their teaching were more likely to emphasize meaning and understanding, encourage student autonomy and persistence, and instruct students in higher-order cognitive strategies.

Implications to Think About

Assessment should be aligned with instruction that takes place during a unit. Using assessment data to inform instruction can make that instruction more responsive to student needs and ensure that every student gains the depth of knowledge and skill necessary. Formative assessment informs teachers of student progress toward learning goals and allows them to modify instruction as needed to improve achievement. Noticeably, the teacher:

- Embeds formative assessment in the learning process

- Shares learning goals with students

- Helps students know and recognize the standards

- Provides feedback students can use to identify ways to improve

- Commits to the idea that every student can improve

- Reviews students' performance and reflects with them on their progress

Ongoing assessment may include informal conversations with and observations of students, open-ended problems that reveal students' understandings and misunderstandings, and traditional paper-and-pencil tests. Teachers should choose the type of assessment to use based on learner and instructional needs. For example, knowing that students often omit finding common denominators when adding fractions aids instruction, and knowing that students can add fractions correctly is critical before moving on to the next topic. Teachers will not always have all the answers and need to be open to students' discoveries of novel approaches and unique understandings of the material.

Many types of assessment, including journaling and creating portfolios, involve student self-monitoring. Reflective self-assessment helps students to be more aware of their learning and to understand their strengths and weaknesses. By examining these self-assessments, teachers will also have a better understanding of individual needs. Self-assessment thus serves a personal metacognitive goal of monitoring individual progress as well as a group goal of improving instruction.

Resources for Learning More

Black, P., Harrison, C., Lee, C., Marshall, B., & William, D. (2003). *Assessment for learning: Putting it into practice.*

Fisher, D., & Frey, N. (2007). *Checking for understanding: Formative assessment techniques for your classroom.*

Gaddy, B. B., Dean, C. B., & Kendall, J. S. (2002). *Noteworthy perspectives: Keeping the focus on learning.*

Glatthorn, A. (with Bragaw, D., Dawkins, K., & Parker, J.). (1998). *Performance assessment and standards-based curricula: The achievement cycle.*

Heritage, M. (2007, October). "Formative assessment: What do teachers need to know and do?"

McMillan, J. H. (Ed.). (2007). *Formative classroom assessment: Theory into practice.*

National Mathematics Advisory Panel. (2008). *Foundations for success: The final report of the National Mathematics Advisory Panel.*

Stepanek, J., & Jarrett, D. (1997). *Assessment strategies to inform science and mathematics instruction: It's just good teaching.*

Stiggins, R. (2005, December). "From formative assessment to assessment for learning: A path to success in standards-based schools."

Svedkauskaite, A., & McNabb, M. (2005). *Critical issue: Multiple dimensions of assessment that support student progress in science and mathematics.*

What impact does teacher content knowledge have on instruction?

Research and Ideas to Know About

Teachers need a deep understanding of the mathematics they teach—concepts, practices, principles, representations, and applications—to support effective instruction. A teacher's conceptual understanding of mathematics affects classroom instruction directly and positively. Content knowledge influences the decisions teachers make about classroom instruction.

Differences in teaching styles between teachers with a rich background in mathematics and those without are very evident. When teachers possess explicit and well-integrated content knowledge, they feel free to teach dynamically with many representations of the same concept, and they encourage student comments and questions. Teachers with more limited content knowledge may depend too heavily on textbooks for explanations of mathematical principles. This often results in controlled classroom environments in which students work individually at their seats, with mathematics portrayed as a set of static facts and procedures.

A close examination of mathematics teaching styles has revealed that teachers with less content knowledge emphasize algorithms and procedures more often. Although teachers with deeper content knowledge teach these same skills, they also engage their students in forming a conceptual understanding of mathematics. When students understand the concepts behind mathematics, they can use mathematics more successfully and demonstrate higher achievement on assessments.

Teachers should be familiar with common misunderstandings students have about mathematical concepts, such as confusing the least common multiple with the greatest common factor. Teachers' own mathematics knowledge should be deep enough to help anticipate these misunderstandings.

Teachers should use their knowledge of mathematics to clarify concepts during instruction and to recognize students' valid alternative problem-solving methods and solutions.

> Mathematics teachers with deep content knowledge are able to teach rich mathematical content to all students.

Implications to Think About

Secondary teachers of mathematics should have degrees in mathematics and be state certified, licensed, or both. All mathematics teachers should have a deep understanding of mathematics content. NCLB addresses this concern with its requirement that all teachers be "highly qualified." Additional teacher preparation courses should focus on the most effective pedagogical methods for building mathematical concepts in children, such as teaching with mathematical and technological tools, allowing students to work collaboratively to solve problems, representing mathematics concepts in various ways, and linking mathematics to other content areas.

Mathematics teachers with deep content knowledge are able to teach rich mathematical content to all students and analyze student work for evidence of conceptual misunderstandings. Content knowledge allows mathematics teachers to:

- Present topics in a real-life context

- Model content in a word-problem format so students will become accustomed to the way mathematics is commonly encountered in the real world

- Link mathematics to other content areas

- Relate learning mathematics to an understanding of technology, personal and social perspectives, historical issues, and cultural values

Skilled mathematics teachers use their knowledge to help students attain a deep understanding of mathematical concepts through activities with manipulatives and other mathematical tools. They encourage the strategic use of technology, such as calculators and computers, so that students can spend more time working on higher-order problems. They also encourage students to participate in mathematical games. Such teachers give students the opportunity to use mathematics to answer real questions, and they develop students' abilities to both estimate and evaluate the rationality of answers. These opportunities for sense making are essential for deep understanding.

Resources for Learning More

Ball, D. L, Lubienski, S., & Mewborn, D. (2001). "Research on teaching mathematics: The unsolved problem of teachers' mathematical knowledge."

Hill, H. C., Rowan, B., & Loewenberg Ball, D. (2005, Summer). "Effects of teachers' mathematical knowledge for teaching on student achievement."

Kilpatrick, J., Swafford, J., & Findell, B. (Eds.). (2001). *Adding it up: Helping children learn mathematics.*

Ma, L. (1999). *Knowing and teaching elementary mathematics: Teachers' understanding of fundamental mathematics in China and the United States.*

National Commission on Mathematics and Science Teaching for the 21st Century. (2000). *Before it's too late: A report to the nation from the National Commission on Mathematics and Science Teaching for the 21st Century.*

National Council of Teachers of Mathematics. (2000). *Principles and standards for school mathematics.*

National Mathematics Advisory Panel. (2008). *Foundations for success: The final report of the National Mathematics Advisory Panel.*

U.S. Department of Education. (2004, March). *Fact sheet: New No Child Left Behind flexibility: Highly qualified teachers.*

2

What impact does teacher pedagogical knowledge have on instruction?

Research and Ideas to Know About

Pedagogical knowledge means understanding the methods and strategies of teaching. Specific methods or strategies that have been proven to work well in one content area, such as mathematics, are referred to as *pedagogical content knowledge.* This knowledge includes knowing what teaching strategies best fit the content and, likewise, knowing how elements of the content can be organized for better teaching. This knowledge differs from the knowledge of a disciplinary expert and also from the general pedagogical knowledge shared by teachers across disciplines. According to the NCTM *Principles and Standards for School Mathematics,* "effective teaching requires knowing and understanding mathematics, students as learners, and pedagogical strategies" (2000, p. 17).

Strong teacher content knowledge alone does not increase student knowledge, nor does using effective pedagogical methods without adequate content knowledge. In fact, rather than improve student achievement, using either alone may actually reinforce student misconceptions. Despite significant changes throughout society over time, teaching methods in most mathematics classes have remained relatively unchanged. Many students spend much of their time on basic computational skills rather than engaging in mathematically rich problem-solving experiences. The most direct route to improving mathematics achievement for all students is through mathematics teaching that uses multiple pedagogical methods.

Extensive research has focused on the influence of (1) teacher characteristics (educational background and years of experience), (2) professional development (training to support classroom practices), and (3) classroom practices (small-group instruction and hands-on learning) on student achievement. Research shows that while all three components influence student achievement, the most influential factor is classroom practices. A principal message cited in the final report of the National Mathematics Advisory Panel indicates that instructional practice should be informed by high-quality research, professional judgment, and teacher experience.

Common mathematics teaching strategies, such as the use of worksheets and a heavy emphasis on computational fluency, are not as effective as engaging students in higher-order thinking skills and hands-on learning activities. Professional development tailored to increase teacher repertoires of classroom instructional practices—coupled with knowledge of mathematics content—increases student academic performance.

Despite significant changes throughout society over time, teaching methods in most mathematics classes have remained unchanged.

Implications to Think About

Effective mathematics teachers employ a large repertoire of instructional methods, strategies, and models to produce more successful learners. Different instructional methods accomplish different learning goals for different students. Teachers should carefully select and plan classroom experiences to provide meaningful mathematics learning opportunities for their increasingly diverse student population. Highly effective mathematics teachers:

- Have a deep knowledge of subject matter, which enables them to draw on that knowledge with flexibility

- Encourage all students to learn for understanding

- Foster healthy skepticism

- Allow for, recognize, and build on differences in learning styles, multiple intelligences, and abilities

- Carefully align curriculum, assessment, and high standards

- Conduct interim assessments of students' progress and use the results to improve instruction

- Measure instructional effectiveness through student performance and achievement

- Use a problem-solving approach

- Hold high expectations for all students

Teachers acquire and enhance their pedagogical skills through training, mentoring, collaborating with peers, and practicing. To change the way they teach, mathematics teachers must receive first-hand opportunities to learn in different ways. They need to observe, practice, and refine high-quality teaching to master the art of teaching mathematics well. As teachers' pedagogical content knowledge increases within the context of a strong mathematical content knowledge, their ability to influence student learning also increases.

Resources for Learning More

Banilower, E. R., Boyd, S. E., Pasley, J. D., & Weiss, I. R. (2006). *Lessons from a decade of mathematics and science reform: A capstone report for the local systemic change through teacher enhancement initiative.*

Ma, L. (1999). *Knowing and teaching elementary mathematics: Teachers' understanding of fundamental mathematics in China and the United States.*

Martin, T. S. (Ed.). (2007). *Mathematics teaching today: Improving practice, improving student learning.*

Marzano, R. J., Pickering, D. J., & Pollock, J. E. (2001). *Classroom instruction that works: Research-based strategies for increasing student achievement.*

National Commission on Mathematics and Science Teaching for the 21st Century. (2000). *Before it's too late: A report to the nation from the National Commission on Mathematics and Science Teaching for the 21st Century.*

National Council of Teachers of Mathematics. (2000). *Principles and standards for school mathematics.*

National Mathematics Advisory Panel. (2008). *Foundations for success: The final report of the National Mathematics Advisory Panel.*

Shulman, L. S. (1986, February). "Those who understand: Knowledge growth in teaching."

Wenglinsky, H. (2000). *How teaching matters: Bringing the classroom back into discussions of teacher quality.*

2

How do teacher attitudes about mathematics learning impact student achievement?

Research and Ideas to Know About

Educational change, just like the success or failure of the education process, depends on what teachers do and think. Teachers mediate between the learner and the subject to be learned; consequently, teachers' beliefs, attitudes, and expectations have a major influence on student achievement. The study of teachers' instructional beliefs and attitudes, and their influence on instructional practice, has gained momentum since the late 1990s.

> A teacher's attitude affects students' daily activities as well as their performance expectations.

A teacher's attitude affects students' daily activities as well as their performance expectations. Teachers who believe it is important for students to learn mathematics with understanding embrace the use of investigations, mathematical discourse, and appropriate mathematical notation and vocabulary. Because a teacher's beliefs influence his or her instructional decisions, pedagogical choices vary among teachers and result in diverse student achievements. A teacher's belief in a balance of whole-class, individual, and small-group work on challenging and interesting problems contributes to improved student achievement.

Teachers who believe in the importance of providing all students the opportunity to learn mathematics with understanding employ strategies that promote student engagement in problem solving. They encourage students to make, test, and revise conjectures and to support their reasoning with evidence. In contrast, teachers who believe that computational prowess is the most important component of mathematics typically demonstrate procedures and provide students time in which to practice those steps. Students who experience a problem-solving approach to the teaching and learning of mathematics consistently outperform students in classrooms that focus on skills and procedures.

Implications to Think About

Teachers' decisions and actions in the classroom directly affect how students will learn mathematics. Teachers need to understand the big ideas of mathematics and be able to represent mathematics as a coherent and connected enterprise.

Student attitudes toward mathematics correlate strongly with their teacher's ability to help students clarify concepts and generate a sense of continuity between the mathematics topics in the curriculum. Effective mathematics teachers approach the content from a more holistic level of understanding. The development of students' positive attitudes in mathematics is directly linked to their participation in activities that involve both quality mathematics and classroom communication. Students who have positive interactions with their mathematics teachers tend to have high confidence in their ability to do mathematics. The attitude of the mathematics teacher is a critical ingredient in building an environment that promotes problem solving and makes students feel comfortable talking about mathematics.

While some mathematics teachers have beliefs that will positively affect their students' learning and achievement, others need to change their attitudes and expectations so that their students can appreciate and understand mathematics. These teachers would benefit from professional development that starts with examining the influence of teacher beliefs, attitudes, and expectations on learning and achievement; includes a self-examination tool; and incorporates communities of practice for ongoing mentoring and support. Teachers' beliefs and practices change when they have opportunities to reflect on innovative, reform-oriented curricula, their students' mathematical thinking, or aspects of their teaching.

Resources for Learning More

Fullan, M. G. (2001). *The new meaning of educational change.*

Handal, B. (2003). "Teachers' mathematical beliefs: A review."

National Council of Teachers of Mathematics. (2000). *Principles and standards for school mathematics.*

Philipp, R. A. (2007). "Mathematics teachers' beliefs and affect."

Stigler, J. W., & Hiebert, J. (1999). *The teaching gap: Best ideas from the world's teachers for improving education in the classroom.*

2

What are the characteristics of effective professional development for mathematics?

Research and Ideas to Know About

Improving teacher quality is the key to increasing student learning. Teacher preparation must do more than transmit discrete skills and techniques to educators and then expect them to instruct students. Research clearly shows that effective professional development must be of adequate duration and must address subject matter and teaching methods.

A growing consensus about effective professional development is that it is most powerful when embedded in teachers' daily work life to create a collaborative culture of inquiry about student understanding. In such an environment, teachers learn new content and related teaching practices, apply them in the classroom, and reflect on the results.

In this approach, discussion about teaching and learning is guided by:

- State and national standards that identify the most important content

- Collected data about student learning (for example, performance assessments, observations and interviews, and standardized test results)

- Teachers' own inquiries about practice (for example, action research and study groups)

As teachers build professional communities, they reduce professional isolation. The most effective schools have strong professional communities, characterized by ongoing collegial and collaborative inquiry into practice. Teaching improves in schools that have cultures of collegiality, experimentation, and risk taking.

In some districts, schools provide opportunities for expert, novice, and preservice teachers to collaboratively study teaching and learning with university faculty and teacher leaders. In such settings, school and university educators partner to improve classroom practices.

Although NCLB requires districts and schools to integrate professional development plans with their school improvement plans, the effect of this approach on student learning remains unclear. Schools and districts that lack the capacity to apply knowledge about effective professional development may need additional assistance.

> "The quality of the outcomes for any school system is essentially the sum of the quality of the instruction that its teachers deliver."
>
> —Barber & Mourshed, 2007, p. 26

Implications to Think About

The five major purposes of professional development for teachers are (1) developing awareness, (2) building knowledge, (3) translating knowledge into practice, (4) practicing teaching, and (5) encouraging self-reflection. The following strategies each address one or more of these purposes:

- *Immersion in mathematics*—engaging in solving mathematics problems as learners

- *Study groups*—engaging in regular collaborative interactions around topics identified by the group to examine new information, reflect on classroom practice, and analyze data

- *Case discussions*—discussing problems and issues illustrated in written narratives or videotapes of classroom events

- *Examining student work*—looking at student products to understand their thinking in order to select the most appropriate instructional strategies and materials (scoring assessments can lead to the same outcome)

- *Action research*—looking at one's own teaching and students' learning through descriptive reporting, purposeful conversation, collegial sharing, and critical reflection

- *Curriculum implementation*—learning, using, and refining specific curriculum materials to build understanding

- *Curriculum development and adaptation*—creating new instructional materials and strategies or adapting existing ones to better meet the learning needs of students

- *Coaching and mentoring*—working regularly with another teacher at the same or greater level of expertise to improve teaching and learning

- *Lesson study*—designing, implementing, testing, and improving one or several lessons over long periods, ranging from several months to a year

- *Blogging*—reflecting on practice, gaining worldwide input to teaching and problem-solving strategies, or both

To engage in this kind of professional development, policymakers at all levels need to support high-quality programs. In turn, teachers need administrator support, time to work with colleagues, and access to resources such as research and outside expertise. For teacher learning and student learning to become priorities, school structure and the policies affecting schools must address professional development needs.

Resources for Learning More

Chicago Lesson Study Group. (2009). *Chicago lesson study group.*

Darling-Hammond, L., & Richardson, N. (2009, February). "Teacher learning: What matters?"

Fernandez, C. (n.d.). *Lesson study research group.*

Garet, M. S., Porter, A. C., Desimone, L., Birman, B. F., & Yoon, K. S. (2001, Winter). "What makes professional development effective? Results from a national sample of teachers."

Jackson, C. K., & Bruegmann, E. (2009). *Teaching students and teaching each other: The importance of peer learning for teachers.*

Lester, F. K. (Ed.). (2007). *Second handbook of research on mathematics teaching and learning.*

Loucks-Horsley, S., Stiles, K., Mundry, S., Love, N., & Hewson, P. W. (Eds.). (1998). *Designing professional development for teachers of science and mathematics.*

Mewborn, D. S. (2003). "Teachers, teachers' knowledge, and their professional development."

National Council of Supervisors of Mathematics. (2009). *Report summary service.*

Smith, M. S. (2001). *Practice-based professional development for teachers of mathematics.*

Snow-Renner, R., & Lauer, P. A. (2005a). *McREL insights—Professional development analysis.*

Sparks, D., & Hirsh, S. (1997). *A new vision for staff development.*

2

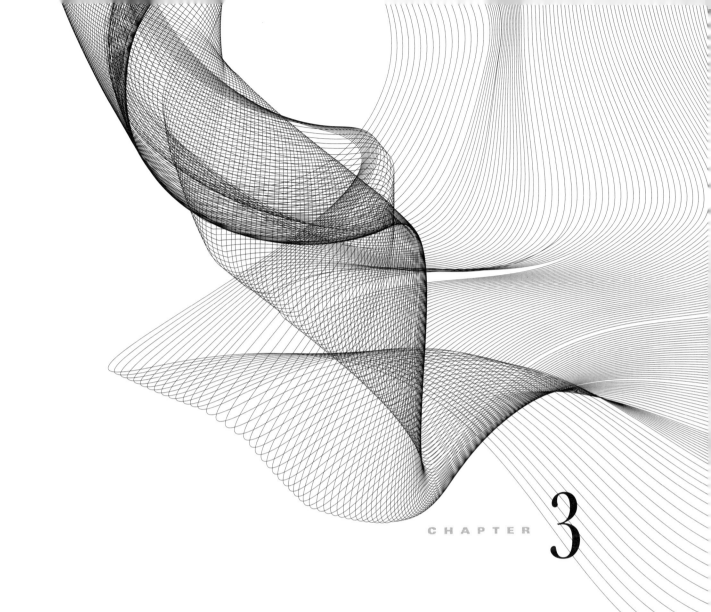

Assessment in Mathematics

Assessment is a complex, systematic process for collecting and interpreting data and is the primary mechanism for feedback on the attainment of standards to students, teachers, parents, school districts, and communities. The NCTM recommends using multiple assessment methods. Since assessments communicate expectations, providing an operational definition of what is important, the *Principles and Standards for School Mathematics* promotes the inclusion of authentic assessments—exercises that closely approximate how mathematics is used in the real world.

The *PSSM* Assessment Principle also recommends measuring both student achievement and opportunity to learn. Interpreted together, this information assists educators and the community at large in assuring that all students can achieve to their potential. Opportunity to Learn measures are important in interpreting both high-stakes individual assessments and international achievement comparisons.

What roles can assessment play in mathematics teaching and learning?

Research and Ideas to Know About

With today's increased accountability for student learning, educators first think about testing as a way to gather feedback about how students are doing. This U.S. emphasis is solidified by NCLB, which requires states to provide report cards that include a host of statistics about school progress. State and other standardized tests provide data on overall school performance and can be valuable program evaluation tools. New approaches to mathematics teaching have expanded the role of assessment to include monitoring student progress and making instructional decisions. Essentially, assessment now plays four roles: (1) evaluate student achievement, (2) evaluate programs, (3) monitor student progress, and (4) make instructional decisions.

Student learning improves when appropriate assessment is a regular part of classroom practice. Using open-ended, inquiry-based problems is a teacher's best chance to assess a student's level of understanding. Research and professional mathematics organizations endorse using multiple and varied measures of assessment, such as performance-based assessment, teacher observations, interviews, student projects, portfolios, and presentations. Such alternative forms of assessment generate the information a teacher needs in order to determine what students are thinking, how they are reasoning, and what steps to take next. The National Mathematics Advisory Panel encourages and recommends regular use of formative assessment. The panel's report also indicates that formative assessment can be especially significant in improving student learning when the teacher understands how to incorporate the data to differentiate instruction.

In the United States, national and state assessments influence what teachers, administrators, and parents value in the classroom. These standardized, norm-referenced assessments tend to favor formats that give the impression there is always one right answer. Research supports that preparing students for such tests can positively affect learning; however, such assessments typically provide only single scores or a small number of scores. Using them to make decisions about individual students is unwise. Educators should take care not to use standardized tests for the wrong purpose. The most useful feedback about individual students comes from ongoing classroom assessments—assessment *for* learning rather than assessment *of* learning.

> Student learning improves when appropriate assessment is a regular part of classroom practice.

Implications to Think About

The sole function of assessment is not accountability; assessment can also help teachers plan curricula and guide daily instruction. Types of assessments include the following:

- Selected-response assessments (such as multiple choice, true/false, and matching) best assess procedural knowledge and factual information. If well-constructed, they can assess complex understandings, but students cannot demonstrate all they know.

- Constructed-response assessments allow students to demonstrate their learning by choosing how to answer the question.

- Performance tasks integrate concepts, skills, facts, reasoning, and problem solving but require extra time to implement and score.

- Observations, checklists, interviews, and portfolios allow students to show the depth of their understanding and can be especially appropriate for English language learners.

- Standardized, norm-referenced tests suggest students' relative strengths and weaknesses across different content strands.

Educators must understand the importance of administering relevant assessments to students and interpreting the data to provide meaningful feedback. The National Council of Supervisors of Mathematics suggests this is accomplished when:

- Content is aligned with instruction and assessment.

- Multiple data sources (such as problem solutions, errors, questions, body language, tests, and homework) are used to make decisions for instruction.

- Summative assessments are aligned with learning goals and designed collaboratively.

- Teachers become proficient in thoughtfully interpreting data from the various models of assessments and learn how to use this evidence to create a more accurate picture of what students know and are able to do; the data also can help educators ensure curricular alignment or determine whether to modify instruction.

Resources for Learning More

Blythe, T., Allen, D., & Powell, B. S. (1999). *Looking together at student work: A companion guide to assessing student learning.*

Bright, G. W., & Joyner, J. M. (Eds.). (1998). *Classroom assessment in mathematics: Views from a National Science Foundation working conference.*

Friedman, M. I., Harwell, D. H., & Schnepel, K. C. (2006). *Effective instruction: A handbook of evidence-based strategies.*

Gaddy, B. B., Dean, C. B., & Kendall, J. S. (2002). *Noteworthy perspectives: Keeping the focus on learning.*

National Council of Supervisors of Mathematics. (2008a). *PRIME leadership framework.*

National Council of Teachers of Mathematics. (1995). *Assessment standards for school mathematics.*

National Mathematics Advisory Panel. (2008). *Foundations for success: The final report of the National Mathematics Advisory Panel.*

National Research Council. (2000). *Inquiry and the national science education standards: A guide for teaching and learning.*

Popham, W. J. (2007). *Classroom assessment: What teachers need to know.*

Stenmark, J. K. (1989). *Assessment alternatives in mathematics: An overview of assessment techniques that promote learning.*

Stiggins, R. (2004). *Student-involved assessment for learning.*

3

How can the use of varied assessments provide important evidence of learning?

Research and Ideas to Know About

Assessment should provide evidence about students' knowledge of mathematics. In order to do so, it must be congruent with state/provincial and local standards and be a good fit with the curriculum and instructional methods a teacher uses. As teachers strive to help their students achieve mathematical literacy (by teaching for understanding and increasing student ability to mathematize problem situations), they need information about students' progress from various sources.

Because different assessment strategies have individual strengths and weaknesses, using a wide variety of classroom assessments gives a better picture of student learning than any single approach. Multiple sources of evidence yield a more comprehensive, ongoing picture of student learning and academic progress and facilitate the exchange of information between teacher and students. This information can also be communicated readily to other members of the school community.

Using multiple types of assessments provides more insight into students' learning because students have more than one way to demonstrate their knowledge and skills. When their achievement is assessed by multiple means, students are more apt to assume greater responsibility for their input into the classroom discourse and to become more reflective. They learn to listen more productively, communicate more clearly, and investigate more deeply. By using specific results to inform their actions, students gain confidence in tackling mathematics problems and in analyzing strategies and solutions. Multiple assessment measures, coupled with students' and teachers' awareness of the importance of assessment to teaching and learning for understanding, can help foster a learning environment centered on continual growth.

> Using multiple types of assessments provides more insight into students' learning because students have more than one way to demonstrate their knowledge and skills.

Implications to Think About

Mathematics teachers should discuss the importance of continuous assessment with students and provide scoring criteria and models of exemplary work for them before they begin a task. Rubrics, used primarily with constructed-response or performance assessments, describe levels of quality for the skills, knowledge, and understandings being assessed. Communicating these expectations to students prior to assigning tasks can promote quality work. Rubrics developed jointly by teachers and students focus learning on understanding, conceptual development, and problem solving.

Some suggest that showing students models of partially completed work, or "anchor" papers that represent all levels of understanding and completion, fosters greater understanding of expectations and, therefore, higher-quality work. When students and teachers collaboratively establish assessment as a tool to inform classroom progress, finding a variety of measures becomes an important component of the instructional process, including making appropriate accommodations for students with special learning needs. Such measures include the following:

- Effective teachers use questioning, classroom observations, interviews, and conferences to facilitate instruction and to inform decision making.

- Careful questioning helps students scaffold their knowledge, focus thinking, and dig deeper into understandings.

- Observations framed around students' grasp of mathematics concepts, their dispositions toward learning, their communication abilities, and their group work contributions help teachers identify appropriate instructional strategies.

- Interviews yield individual insights into a problem, a way of thinking, an orientation to problem solving, and a uniqueness of approach.

- By conferencing together, students and teachers can reflect on a student's learning and current disposition toward mathematics, and set future goals.

- Conversations with peers also augment learning.

Individual self-evaluation through reflection (such as a mathematics autobiography, goal setting, daily evaluations, chronicling of "ah-ha's," record keeping, or journaling) personalizes an activity for students. Through writing in particular, students learn to organize, convey, question, conclude, and defend—these all are mathematics thinking processes. Using multiple means of assessment allows students to diversify their thinking and responses. Real-world problems, computer-based assessment, critical evaluation of mathematical logic, and structured problem-solving tasks stretch student thinking about meaningful mathematics assessment. Teachers need to increase their repertoire of assessment strategies and should have opportunities for ongoing professional development in which they examine an array of student work.

Resources for Learning More

Bush, W. S., & Greer, A. S. (Eds.). (1999). *Mathematics assessment: A practical handbook for grades 9–12.*

Bush, W. S., & Leinwand, S. (Eds.). (2000). *Mathematics assessment: A practical handbook for grades 6–8.*

Clarke, D. (1997). *Constructive assessment in mathematics: Practical steps for classroom teachers.*

Fennema, E., & Romberg, T. A. (Eds.). (1999). *Mathematics classrooms that promote understanding.*

Gaddy, B. B., Dean, C. B., & Kendall, J. S. (2002). *Noteworthy perspectives: Keeping the focus on learning.*

Glandfield, F., Bush, W. S., & Stenmark, J. K. (Eds.). (2003). *Mathematics assessment: A practical handbook for grades K–2.*

Stenmark, J. K., Bush, W. S., & Allen, C. (Eds.). (2001). *Mathematics assessment: A practical handbook for grades 3–5.*

Zemelman, S., Daniels, H., & Hyde, A. (1998). *Best practice: New standards for teaching and learning in America's schools.*

3

How can mathematical thinking be assessed in the classroom?

Mathematical thinking is sometimes defined as "a search for truth or knowledge" or "a systematic investigation of a matter of interest" that embodies the mathematical processes of problem solving, inquiry, reasoning and proof, communication, connections, and representation. These processes are ways of acquiring and using content knowledge.

A task intended to assess mathematical processes should provide opportunities for students to describe the mathematics they used, explain why they proceeded as they did, relate what they did to something they have done previously, and communicate their ideas in a manner most appropriate to them. For example, students might use pictures, graphs, discussions, written reports, or electronic displays.

Often, good instructional tasks are also effective assessment pieces. Assessment that enhances mathematics learning becomes a routine part of ongoing classroom activity rather than an interruption; opportunities for informal assessment occur naturally in every lesson. Simple procedures like listening to students as they work, observing them, accumulating their work over time (via portfolios, for example), and interviewing them are some of the informal measures that can provide valuable information to the teacher for instructional decision making and to students for learning.

Formal assessments often come in the form of performance tasks or student-constructed response items. Formal assessment items can be selected or created in ways that enable students to demonstrate what they know and can do rather than what they do not know. Performance tasks might include projects or investigations that students present to their classmates as presentations or displays. For example, students could explore their neighborhood, looking for a mathematics problem, and then create a display of the problem and its solution. Or students could prepare a PowerPoint or other multimedia presentation on some aspect of a concept they just studied or a problem they liked.

Student-constructed response items allow students to show their solution processes and explain their thinking. Rubrics, scoring guides, and quality examples should be shared with students in advance to communicate performance expectations. Effective scoring guides and rubrics give students credit for their insight about a task, their reasoning, the clarity of their communication, and the appropriateness of their representations, as well as for the accuracy of their results.

In assessing applications and other problem-based contexts for doing mathematics, we need to be able to identify essential, embedded mathematics content.

Implications to Think About

Assessing understanding requires multiple measures—both informal and formal—over time. Teachers need to use assessment techniques that measure students':

- Use of mathematics to make sense of complex situations

- Work on extended investigations

- Ability to formulate and refine hypotheses; collect and organize information; explain a concept orally or in writing; and work with poorly defined problems or problems with multiple answers, similar to those encountered in real life

- Use of mathematical processes in the context of many kinds of problems rather than in isolation

- Understanding of mathematical concepts

- Ability to define and formulate problems, question possible solutions, and look at all possibilities

- Progress over time

Because we are striving to assess higher-order thinking, identifying the components of the mathematical thinking processes is important. In assessing applications and other problem-based contexts for doing mathematics, we need to be able to identify essential, embedded mathematics content and have some idea about how the context and content interact with performance.

Resources for Learning More

Bush, W. S., & Greer, A. S. (Eds.). (1999). *Mathematics assessment: A practical handbook for grades 9–12.*

Bush, W. S., & Leinwand, S. (Eds.). (2000). *Mathematics assessment: A practical handbook for grades 6–8.*

Clarke, D. (1997). *Constructive assessment in mathematics: Practical steps for classroom teachers.*

Glandfield, F., Bush, W. S., & Stenmark, J. K. (Eds.). (2003). *Mathematics assessment: A practical handbook for grades K–2.*

Lazear, D. (2004). *Higher-order thinking the multiple intelligences way.*

National Council of Teachers of Mathematics. (1995). *Assessment standards for school mathematics.*

Shafer, M. C., & Romberg, T. A. (1999). "Assessment in classrooms that promote understanding."

Stenmark, J. K., Bush, W. S., & Allen, C. (Eds.). (2001). *Mathematics assessment: A practical handbook for grades 3–5.*

Svedkauskaite, A., & McNabb, M. (2005). *Critical issue: Multiple dimensions of assessment that support student progress in science and mathematics.*

3

What do national and international assessments tell us about teaching and learning mathematics?

Research and Ideas to Know About

Mathematical competency is necessary to prepare an educated citizenry for democracy, the changing economy and workplace, and national security.

Results on U.S. and international assessments provide a measure by which to compare U.S. student achievement in mathematics across states and nations. These results have forced mathematics educators, mathematicians, policymakers, and community members to examine the delivery system in preK–12 mathematics education. Mathematical competency is necessary to prepare an educated citizenry for democracy, the changing economy and workplace, and national security.

The results of the third Trends in International Mathematics and Science Study showed that American students were not performing at acceptable levels in mathematics compared with their counterparts in other countries. Notably, in the second TIMSS-repeat study 86 percent of eighth-graders reported that they worked on their own from worksheets or textbooks "almost always" or "pretty often" during mathematics lessons, which was higher than the international average of 59 percent. In 2003, PISA reported that fifteen-year-olds' performance in mathematics literacy and problem solving ranked lower than the average performance for most industrialized countries.

Concerns about performance on U.S. and international assessments sparked the formation of the National Mathematics Advisory Panel in 2006. The panel's twenty-month study focused primarily on school algebra and the preparation needed in grades preK–8 to ensure readiness for an authentic algebra course by grade 9. Released in 2008, the panel's main findings and recommendations addressed the areas of curricular content, learning processes, teachers and teacher education, instructional practices, instructional materials, assessment, and research policies and mechanisms.

Disaggregated National Assessment of Educational Progress (NAEP) results are instructive. Gender differences are statistically insignificant except at grade 12, where males outperform females in mathematics. This difference can probably be attributed to the fact that males tend to complete advanced courses at a higher rate than females. Significant performance differences exist across ethnic groups at all grade levels, even though the scores for each ethnic group have increased over the years. Factors such as socioeconomic status, home environment, and educational opportunities must be considered when interpreting the achievement differences among ethnic groups. The National Mathematics Advisory Panel recommended in 2008 that NAEP and state assessments be improved in quality and emphasize the most important topics leading to algebra.

Implications to Think About

U.S. school districts should find national and state standards instructive as they develop local standards, documents, and procedures. The challenge is to limit the number of topics addressed without compromising the integrity of a demanding curriculum. Introducing more complex topics earlier allows students to gradually be exposed to the rigorous underlying concepts of algebra, geometry, discrete mathematics, and statistics. Attention to standards allows curriculum developers to create coherent, articulated curricular programs.

There is a connection between what is taught and how well it is taught. Student performance improves when students are taught to seek conceptual understanding rather than simply follow procedures. Lesson design should reflect effective instructional strategies and should relate the various mathematical strands.

International comparisons indicate that the most powerful instrument for change in student performance is improved teaching. A highly effective level of teaching:

- Requires a deep knowledge of the mathematics being taught, as well as an understanding of what is most important to learn and what is most difficult to understand

- Engages students not only in the computational aspects of mathematics, but also in its more meaningful conceptual aspects

- Involves problem solving as students learn and apply the lesson content

- Insists that all students learn at high levels

- Demands high-quality professional development opportunities to keep teachers current in content, pedagogy, and assessment

- Includes time to share with colleagues, which is critical in developing a learning community and professionalism among teachers

- Uses the same kinds of mathematics tasks students in high-performing countries engage in

Ongoing, planned professional development enables teachers to achieve high levels of teaching. Designers of professional development for U.S. teachers could benefit from studying models used in other countries.

Resources for Learning More

Gonzales, P., Calsyn, C., Jocelyn, L., Mak, K., Kastberg, D., Arafeh, S., et al. (2000). *Pursuing excellence: Comparison of international eighth-grade mathematics and science achievement from a U.S. perspective, 1995 and 1999.*

Institute of Education Sciences. (n.d.). *Fast facts.*

Jamison, D. T., Jamison, E. A., Woessmann, L., & Hanushek, E. (2008, Spring). "Education and economic growth."

Mullis, I. V. S., Martin, M. O., & Foy, P. (with Olson, J. F., Preuschoff, C., Erberber, E., Arora, A., & Galia, J.). (2008). *TIMSS 2007 international mathematics report: Findings from IEA's Trends in International Mathematics and Science Study at the Fourth and Eighth Grades.*

Mullis, I. V. S., Martin, M. O., Gonzalez, E. J., Gregory, K. D., Garden, R. A., O'Connor, K. M., et al. (2000). *TIMSS 1999 International Mathematics Report: Findings from IEA's Repeat of the Third International Mathematics and Science Study at the Eighth Grade.*

National Assessment of Educational Progress. (2007). *The nation's report card.*

National Mathematics Advisory Panel. (2008). *Foundations for success: The final report of the National Mathematics Advisory Panel.*

Organisation for Economic Co-operation and Development. (2004). *Learning for tomorrow's world: First results from PISA 2003.*

Provasnik, S., Gonzales, P., & Miller, D. (2009). *U.S. performance across international assessments of student achievement: Special supplement to the condition of education 2009.*

Stigler, J. W., & Hiebert, J. (1999). *The teaching gap: Best ideas from the world's teachers for improving education in the classroom.*

Trends in International Mathematics and Science Study. (2007). *Mathematics achievement of fourth- and eighth-graders between 1995 and 2007.*

3

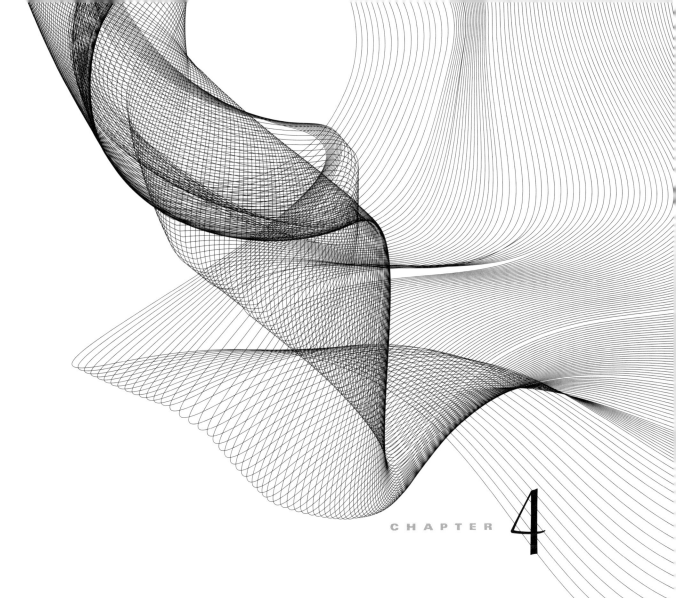

CHAPTER 4

Mathematics Curriculum

The content standards in the NCTM *Principles and Standards for School Mathematics* define the content of instruction, outlining what every student should know and be able to do. The district curriculum, however, describes how that content is organized. The curriculum also includes emphases and perspectives placed on the content, creating a map for educators to use in designing classroom experiences for students.

Recognizing that the intent of content standards is to present a goal for all students, teachers must make curriculum decisions that accommodate a wide variety of learning styles, backgrounds, and interests. When educators use multiple means of addressing individual standards, all learners have an opportunity to access common content.

What is the importance of standards-based curricula in mathematics?

Research and Ideas to Know About

Standards are a set of expectations for what students will learn. Standards have grown increasingly pervasive since the 1990s. Close to 100 percent of all U.S. states and territories are joining the Common Core State Standards initiative. The goal of this initiative is to define standards that are not only based on research and evidence, but are also internationally benchmarked, aligned with college and workforce expectations, and made rigorous in both content and skills.

A standards-based curriculum arises from a given set of standards and provides the details of how students should progress through various learning experiences in order to meet them. The Curriculum Principle of *PSSM* states, "A curriculum is more than a collection of activities: it must be coherent, focused on important mathematics, and well articulated across the grades" (2000, p. 14).

Standards are most visible in American classrooms as curriculum. Standards-based mathematics curricula can increase students' understanding of mathematics, but programs must be implemented as they were designed. Taking the recommended amount of time to work through the scope and sequence, teachers should use all of the essential features of standards-based programs defined in the *PSSM* Curriculum Principle. These features include promoting classroom discourse, presenting mathematics skills in the context of problem solving, and applying learning to real-life situations.

Standards-based curricula and instructional guidelines can positively influence student achievement and can influence teachers to adopt research-informed instructional practices. Additionally, standards-based accountability systems and assessments exert strong influence on classroom instruction. Research shows that students at risk of failing would benefit from more research-informed instruction, provided that access is assured.

> Standards are most visible in American classrooms as curriculum.

Implications to Think About

Standards-based curricula are powerful means of implementing standards, but teachers who previously felt effective using traditional practices might need reassurance, coaching, and guidance during the implementation of a new standards-based curriculum. Programs that embed skill development in problem solving, games, real-world situations, and other contexts are unfamiliar to many educators, and the path of skill development in such materials is not always obvious at a glance. Teachers need opportunities to experience sample lessons themselves and to try out multiple lessons while monitoring student learning.

Teachers who believe that skills are learned through repeated practice might be tempted to supplement a standards-based program with unrelated skills practice. Similarly, some teachers might be more comfortable with a direct instructional approach than with problem solving. Because one characteristic of standards-based learning is coherence, teachers should follow the intended curriculum; otherwise, students are at a disadvantage. Good curriculum materials build in teacher support.

Initial and ongoing professional development are crucial for teachers implementing standards-based curriculum. In addition, administrators and policymakers must find ways to make instruction equitable among diverse groups of students. If standards really mean high expectations for all students to learn, classroom practice must provide avenues for all students to succeed in both learning and using content materials. Students who have no opportunity to learn the content in standards cannot reach those standards.

Resources for Learning More

Council of Chief State School Officers. (2009). *Common core state standards initiative.*

Hiebert, J. (1999, January). "Relationships between research and the NCTM standards: An introduction."

Hiebert, J., Carpenter, T. P., Fennema, E., Fuson, K. C., Wearne, D., Murray, H., et al. (1997). *Making sense: Teaching and learning mathematics with understanding.*

Hirsch, C. R. (Ed.). (2007). *Perspectives on design and development of school mathematics curricula.*

Martin, T. S. (Ed.). (2007). *Mathematics teaching today: Improving practice, improving student learning.*

National Council of Teachers of Mathematics. (2000). *Principles and standards for school mathematics.*

Palacios, L. (2005). *Critical issue: Mathematics education in the era of NCLB—principles and standards.*

Schmidt, W., Houang, R., & Cogan, L. (2002, Summer). "A coherent curriculum: The case of mathematics."

Senk, S. L., & Thompson, D. R. (Eds.). (2003). *Standards-based school mathematics curricula: What are they? What do students learn?*

Sleeter, C. E. (2005). *Un-standardizing curriculum: Multicultural teaching in the standards-based classroom.*

Snow-Renner, R., & Lauer, P. A. (2005b). *McREL insights—Standards-based education: Putting research into practice.*

4

How do we determine what students should know and be able to do in mathematics?

Research and Ideas to Know About

There is a general consensus that mathematics is a "gatekeeper" discipline. Students who demonstrate proficiency in mathematics are more likely to take advanced courses in high school and to continue on to postsecondary education. Studies indicate that the highest level of mathematics studied in high school has a strong correlation to the completion of a bachelor's degree. Completing a course beyond Algebra 2 more than doubles the odds of bachelor's degree completion. NCLB requires states to set standards to achieve universal proficiency. The final report of the National Mathematics Advisory Panel provides further guidance regarding benchmarks for preK–8 students and major topics of school algebra. The question of what mathematics all students should know and be able to do is, therefore, extremely significant.

PSSM identifies the "big ideas" in mathematics and how these concepts develop throughout the grade bands.

This question led to the development of the NCTM *Curriculum and Evaluation Standards for School Mathematics* in 1989 and its 2000 revision, *Principles and Standards for School Mathematics*. This question was further studied when the National Mathematics Advisory Panel was established by executive order in 2006. The standards in these documents and the recommendations from this panel reflect input received from mathematicians, mathematics educators, parents, business leaders, and teachers about what content and processes all students should know and be able to do in order to be mathematically literate and prepared for the twenty-first-century workplace.

PSSM is not the traditional laundry list of topics you might see in the table of contents of a mathematics text; rather, it identifies the "big ideas" in mathematics and how these concepts develop throughout the grade bands. The content areas in which all students must become proficient include numbers and operations, algebra, geometry, measurement, and data analysis and probability. The process skills critical to achieving mathematics proficiency include problem solving, reasoning and proof, communication, connections, and representation. Research indicates that when mathematics procedural skills are learned in the context of real-world content, students typically demonstrate a deeper understanding of mathematics than when those skills are practiced in isolation.

The standards also set an expectation that all students learn to value mathematics, become confident in their ability to do mathematics, become mathematical problem solvers, and learn to communicate and reason mathematically. These mathematical habits of mind apply not only to using the content and procedures of mathematics, but also to acting as a responsible citizen.

Implications to Think About

In a standards-based curriculum, teachers design learning experiences to enable all of their students to reach the level of understanding or skill described by applicable standards. One mathematical area that demands more attention is *number sense*—how numerical quantities are constructed and how they relate to one another. When instruction is rooted in daily experiences and connected to prior learning, students begin to think mathematically and to look for and analyze patterns in mathematics. Additionally, students need to make estimates, check the reasonableness of their answers, and demonstrate computational fluency in problem solving.

Learning geometry incorporates concrete models, drawings, and dynamic software. Studying measurement provides opportunities to learn about other areas of mathematics, including number operations, geometric ideas, statistical concepts, and notions of functions. Data analysis and probability are essential for informed citizenship. All students must formulate questions that can be addressed with data and have opportunities to collect, organize, and display relevant data to answer those questions.

Students should use data analysis and probability to connect mathematics to other subject areas in meaningful rather than contrived ways. They should use multiple representations, and be able to choose the appropriate representation for a particular problem. All students should be engaged in algebraic reasoning—not just manipulating symbols, but actively generating data; representing it in tables, charts, and/or graphs; identifying patterns and relationships; making predictions; and expressing relationships through symbols.

To maximize student learning, teachers should balance inquiry-based learning and direct instruction. Classroom experiences should promote the development of students' reasoning, justification, inquiry, and mathematics content skills. Students should be encouraged to use geometric representations for numeric and algebraic concepts, make and test conjectures, and be able to construct their own proofs.

Resources for Learning More

Collins, A. M. (2000, September 6). "Yours is not to reason why."

Grunow, J. E. (2001). *Planning curriculum in mathematics.*

Hirsch, C. (with Cox, D., Kasmer, L., Madden, S., & Moore, D.). (2007, February). "Some common themes and notable differences across recent national mathematics curriculum documents."

Kilpatrick, J., Swafford, J., & Findell, B. (Eds.). (2001). *Adding it up: Helping children learn mathematics.*

Luft, P., Brown, C. M., & Sutherin, L. J. (2007, July/August). "Are you and your students bored with the benchmarks? Sinking under the standards? Then transform your teaching through transition!"

Mokros, J., Russell, S. J., & Economopoulos, K. (1995). *Beyond arithmetic: Changing mathematics in the elementary classroom.*

National Council of Teachers of Mathematics. (1989). *Curriculum and evaluation standards for school mathematics.*

National Council of Teachers of Mathematics. (2000). *Principles and standards for school mathematics.*

National Mathematics Advisory Panel. (2008). *Foundations for success: The final report of the National Mathematics Advisory Panel.*

Schoenfeld, A. H. (2004, January). "The math wars."

4

What are curriculum coherence and articulation?

Research and Ideas to Know About

Principles and Standards for School Mathematics states that a curriculum is more than a collection of activities; it must be coherent, focused on important mathematics, and well articulated across the grades. A *coherent curriculum* allows students to see how important mathematical ideas build on—or connect with—other ideas, thus enabling them to develop new understandings and skills. An effective mathematics curriculum prepares students for continued study and for solving problems in various settings.

Articulation describes the relationships among elements in a curriculum and ensures connections between lessons, units, courses, and grade levels. Mathematics comprises interconnected topical strands that should be displayed prominently in the curriculum, instructional materials, and lessons. These connections support the increasingly rigorous development of ideas; therefore, a well-articulated curriculum challenges students to learn increasingly sophisticated mathematical ideas.

In studies worldwide, the U.S. curriculum has been characterized as lacking in rigor, focus, and coherence. The proliferation of state-specific standards has served only to exacerbate this problem. An international comparison of textbooks and curriculum guides reveals that U.S. textbooks contain many more topics. Covering so many topics yields disjointed, rather than coherent, learning and does not allow students to develop a deep understanding of the topics covered.

High-stakes assessment and accountability systems have prompted U.S. education leaders to identify important mathematics topics at each level. A state-to-state review of grade-level learning expectations shows vast discrepancies in numbers of topic expectations at given levels. To help teachers and leaders make curricular decisions, in 2006, NCTM released *Curriculum Focal Points for Prekindergarten Through Grade 8 Mathematics: A Quest for Coherence*. Although *PSSM* remains the comprehensive document to identify concepts and skills across grade bands, *Curriculum Focal Points* describes critical "targets" at each grade level and emphasizes the connections within and across mathematical strands.

In 2008, the release of the final report of the National Mathematics Advisory Panel commended *Curriculum Focal Points* as a starting point for a more focused, coherent curriculum but called for even more reduction in topics. The panel recommends a preK–8 curriculum that focuses primarily on preparation for algebra. It cites fluency with whole numbers and fractions and aspects of geometry and measurement as critical building blocks to success in algebra.

A coherent curriculum allows students to see how important mathematical ideas build on—or connect with—other ideas, thus enabling them to develop new understandings and skills. . . . Articulation describes the relationships among elements in a curriculum and ensures connections between lessons, units, courses, and grade levels.

Implications to Think About

Several common practices contribute to a lack of coherence and articulation within a curriculum:

- Emphasis on mastery, using reteaching and repetition

- Overuse of rote memorization

- Content "coverage" by textbooks

- Overly flexible, modular curriculum design that promotes inconsistent instruction

- Lack of district attention to curriculum program development

To achieve coherence and articulation, a curriculum program must:

- Focus on the concepts and skills critical to understanding important mathematical processes and relationships

- Help students develop an understanding of these concepts and skills over several years and in logical ways that recognize intellectual readiness

- Establish explicit connections among the concepts and skills in ways that allow students to see and make those connections

- Assess and diagnose what students understand in order to determine the next steps in instruction

A coherent curriculum typically contains fewer but richer topics that lead to greater depth and persistence of understanding. Content must be sequenced logically so that students accrue the experiences needed to develop understanding and see the relationships among ideas. A well-articulated, coherent curriculum should not only take advantage of important prior knowledge but should also have multiple entry points that allow all students who may have gaps in their prior knowledge to participate and learn rigorous mathematics content. Therefore, teachers must know what students learned in prior grades, what they need to learn in their current grade, and what they will need to be prepared to learn in future grades.

Resources for Learning More

Apthorp, H. S., Bodrova, E., Dean, C. B., & Florian, J. E. (with Gaddy, B. B., Goodwin, B. R., Lauer, P. A., & Snow-Renner, R.). (2001). *Noteworthy perspectives: Teaching to the core—Reading, writing, and mathematics.*

National Council of Teachers of Mathematics. (2000). *Principles and standards for school mathematics.*

National Council of Teachers of Mathematics. (2006). *Curriculum focal points for prekindergarten through grade 8 mathematics: A quest for coherence.*

National Mathematics Advisory Panel. (2008). *Foundations for success: The final report of the National Mathematics Advisory Panel.*

National Research Council. (1999). *Designing mathematics or science curriculum programs: A guide for using mathematics and science education standards.*

Schoenfeld, A. H. (2002, January–February). "Making mathematics work for all children: Issues of standards, testing, and equity."

Stein, M. K., Remillard, J., & Smith, M. S. (2007). "How curriculum influences student learning."

Valverde, G. A., & Schmidt, W. H. (1997, Winter). "Refocusing U.S. math and science education."

What is the importance of reading and writing in the mathematics curriculum?

Research and Ideas to Know About

Reading, writing, and mathematics are—or should be—inseparable. Hands-on mathematics can stimulate curiosity, engage student interest, and build important prior knowledge before students read or write about the topic. The more students know about a topic, the better they comprehend and learn from reading more about it. Prior knowledge is the strongest predictor of students' ability to make inferences from text.

Hands-on mathematics, though, must be combined with minds-on activities. Reading and writing activities can help students analyze, interpret, and communicate mathematical ideas. These skills are needed to evaluate sources of information and the validity of the information itself, a key area of competence for mathematically literate citizens.

Many process skills needed for mathematics are similar to reading skills, and when taught together, they reinforce each other. Examples of common skills are predicting, inferring, communicating, comparing and contrasting, and recognizing cause-and-effect relationships. Characteristics of mathematics texts that students find difficult include word density, direction reading (not only left to right, but also right to left, up and down, and diagonally), symbols, and mathematics-specific vocabulary. To address these, direct instruction is essential. Research continues to reveal that vocabulary knowledge is the single most important factor contributing to reading comprehension.

Teachers who recognize the interrelatedness of mathematics and literacy processes can design instruction that reflects these similarities. *Becoming a Nation of Readers: The Report of the Commission on Reading* suggests that the most logical place for instruction in reading and thinking strategies is within the content areas rather than in separate lessons about reading.

The importance of writing in the mathematics classroom is paramount. During the writing process, students clarify their understanding of mathematics and hone their communication skills. They must organize their ideas and thoughts logically and structure their conclusions coherently. Competency in writing can be accomplished only through active practice; solving mathematics problems is a natural vehicle for increasing students' writing competence.

> Reading and writing activities can help students analyze, interpret, and communicate mathematical ideas.

Implications to Think About

Motivating and engaging students to speak, ask questions, learn new vocabulary, and write down their thoughts comes easily when they are curious, exploring, and engaged in their own mathematics inquiry. Teachers can take advantage of students' innate inquisitiveness to develop language skills while learning mathematics concepts. Integrating literacy activities into mathematics classes helps clarify concepts and can make mathematics more meaningful and interesting. Teachers can use a wide variety of reading sources, including trade books, texts, newspapers, technical manuals, Internet sources, and fiction. Selecting a fiction book with a mathematical theme both provides information and captivates student interest. Fiction works successfully with young learners by embedding cognitive learning in imaginative stories.

Asking students to write mathematics journals about their problem-solving experiences or to articulate and defend their views about mathematics-related issues provides opportunities to clarify their thinking and develop communications skills. Other ways to integrate writing in mathematics are recording and describing situations that involve mathematics, or writing persuasive letters on local or national issues that incorporate mathematics in their arguments, such as a sampling by the Census Bureau. NCTM provides annual lists of outstanding new literature and multimedia materials.

Mathematics instruction is enhanced for ELLs when they can use hands-on materials to ask and answer questions or as visual aids in conversation with teachers and peers. Teachers should provide visual and auditory clues, such as charts with pictures of materials and key procedures; select vocabulary carefully; repeat key words often; and refer to charts with the written words. Students should work in pairs or small groups to facilitate native-language support by peers or instructional aides. Ultimately, strategies that assist ELLs benefit all students.

Mathematics teachers can help all students increase their comprehension of mathematics texts by activating their prior knowledge through brainstorming, discussing the topic, asking questions, and providing analogies. Specific attention to content area vocabulary is essential to enable comprehension of mathematics texts. Simply looking up words in a dictionary does not promote real understanding. Teachers should introduce new vocabulary and use a graphic organizer, a concept or semantic map, or collaborative peer study techniques to develop understanding of new words.

Resources for Learning More

Anderson, R. C., Hiebert, E. H., Scott, J. A., & Wilkinson, I. A. G. (1984). *Becoming a nation of readers: The report of the commission on reading.*

Barton, M. L., & Heidema, C. (2002). *Teaching reading in mathematics: A supplement to* Teaching reading in the content areas: If not me, then who?

Billmeyer, R., & Barton, M. L. (2002). *Teaching reading in the content areas: If not me, then who?*

Buehl, D. (1998, October). "Making math make sense."

Burns, M. (1995). *Writing in math class: A resource for grades 2–8.*

Marzano, R. J. (2004). *Building background knowledge for academic achievement: Research on what works in schools.*

Urquhart, V., & McIver, M. (2005). *Teaching writing in the content areas.*

Wallace, F. H., Clark, K. K., & Cherry, M. L. (2006, September). "How come? What if? So what? Reading in the mathematics classroom."

Wisconsin Department of Public Instruction. (2007). *Adolescent learning toolkit.*

4

What considerations are the most important in selecting textbooks and other materials?

Research and Ideas to Know About

Instructional materials for preK–12 school mathematics include textbooks, manipulative sets, software, CDs, trade books, and other multimedia materials. They are a primary source of classroom mathematics learning as well as teacher professional development, which often is structured around these materials.

In preparation for the final report of the National Mathematics Advisory Panel, the subcommittee on instructional materials looked at the accuracy, length, and coherence of textbooks as well as the sequencing of topics. The committee found that not only are U.S. mathematics textbooks extremely long (ranging from six hundred to nine hundred pages in high school and in excess of seven hundred pages in elementary) compared to those in the high-performing nations, but there were also an unacceptable number of errors and confusing statements and problems. Although the subcommittee recommended that publishers be responsible for having mathematicians review texts before publication, educators should be aware of these concerns and take them into consideration during textbook selection.

A thoughtful, rigorous materials selection process is critical to providing students and teachers with a solid foundation for improving achievement. Four key steps to the textbook selection process are (1) establishing a review/selection committee that includes mathematics teachers, (2) determining selection criteria, (3) selecting an evaluation instrument, and (4) evaluating and selecting materials. The process may be done at the district, school, department, or even classroom level. Most decisions must be ratified by an administrator or school board. Many states review materials and restrict districts and schools to these approved materials.

An important selection criterion is that instructional materials develop the student understanding called for in the standards. Reviewers familiar with the discipline and the standards should also be familiar with what research says works. Quality instructional materials will enhance student understanding; promote students' active involvement; hold high expectations for all students, with guidance for teaching diverse learners; incorporate problem-solving skills; use an appropriate learning sequence; include assessment instruments and methods; and reflect current research in mathematics education.

Investing time and effort in materials selection is important, because the quality of instructional materials relates to student achievement. Teachers also need professional development specific to using the materials. Finally, the effectiveness of the process and the selected materials should be evaluated before the next selection cycle.

> Investing time and effort in materials selection is important, because the quality of instructional materials relates to student achievement.

Implications to Think About

Instructional materials that promote student learning in positive, innovative ways (1) have strong mathematical content; (2) are well organized; (3) contain content that relates to students' experiences and teachers' roles; and (4) provide assessment suggestions. The mathematical content of the materials selected should reflect state or district mathematics standards. The organization of the program should include cohesive units, multiday lessons, and worthwhile tasks that allow students sufficient time to explore and investigate ideas in-depth. Materials should develop students' mathematical understanding and ability and should clearly illustrate connections within mathematics and among other curriculum areas such as language arts, science, history, or art. Problem solving, communication, and reasoning should also be built into the program at all levels.

Instructional materials should give students opportunities to be active, engaged learners, exploring and investigating mathematical ideas, and should provide students with opportunities to communicate orally and in writing not only with one another, but also with the teacher. Quality instructional materials provide suggestions to help students learn. These suggestions should elicit, engage, and challenge students' thinking, explain various methods that give all students the opportunity to learn, and outline possible enriched or advanced work.

Student assessment should be integrated into the instructional program using assessment activities similar to the learning activities. The materials should use multiple means of assessment and suggest ways to assess students individually or in small groups—through observations, oral and written work, student demonstrations or presentations, and student self-assessment. Conceptual understandings and procedural knowledge should be frequently assessed through tasks that ask students to apply mathematical knowledge in novel situations.

High-quality instructional materials alone cannot ensure that learning takes place. Teachers must use the materials appropriately in classroom activities and be knowledgeable about research-based materials. The What Works Clearinghouse (http://ies.ed.gov/ncee/wwc) and Doing What Works (http://dww.ed.gov) websites are resources that feature scientific evidence of what works in education.

Resources for Learning More

Education Development Center. (2005). *The K–12 mathematics curriculum center.*

Gersten, R., Beckmann, S., Clarke, B., Foegen, A., Marsh, L., Star, J. R., et al. (2009). *Assisting students struggling with mathematics: Response to intervention (RtI) for elementary and middle schools.*

Goldsmith, L. T., Mark, J., & Kantrov, I. (2000). *Choosing a standards-based mathematics curriculum.*

Hellwig, S. J., Monroe, E. E., & Jacobs, J. S. (2000, November). "Making informed choices: Selecting children's trade books for mathematics instruction."

Institute of Education Sciences. (n.d.). *What works clearinghouse.*

Kulm, G., Roseman, J. E., & Treistman, M. (1999, July/August). "A benchmarks-based approach to textbook evaluation."

National Research Council. (1999). *Designing mathematics or science curriculum programs: A guide for using mathematics and science education standards.*

Palacios, L. (2005). *Critical issue: Mathematics education in the era of NCLB—principles and standards.*

Siegler, R. S., Fristedt, B., Williams, V., Arispe, I., Berch, D. B., & Banfield, M. (2008). "Report of the subcommittee on instructional materials."

Tarr, J. E., Reys, B. J., Barker, D. D., & Billstein, R. (2006, August). "Selecting high-quality mathematics textbooks."

U.S. Department of Education. (n.d.). *Doing what works.*

4

In what ways can integrating curriculum enhance learning in mathematics?

Research and Ideas to Know About

In real life, learning experiences are not separated into academic disciplines or subject areas. A student's classroom experiences should mirror this. Interconnections among the academic disciplines—referred to here as *subject integration*—when emphasized at all grade levels, will support learning by making the mathematics curriculum more meaningful.

Brain research has shown that long-term memory, or true learning, depends on information that makes sense and has meaning. Subject integration helps a student make sense and understand the meaning of new information. Without these connections, students' learning experiences would add up to a collection of miscellaneous topics and unrelated facts. As early as 1938, John Dewey warned that isolation in all forms is to be avoided and that we should strive for connectedness. *Benchmarks for Science Literacy*, from the American Association for the Advancement of Science, states that interconnected knowledge should be designed to "see the relationships among science, mathematics, and technology and between them and other human endeavors" (1993, p. 320).

If the goal is to produce mathematically literate citizens who can apply mathematical thinking in real-life problem solving, then subject integration is essential. Problem-based learning using real-life problems is a powerful motivational tool. When connections extend across curriculum areas, they establish a mental framework that students can recall for future problem solving. This approach helps students see commonalities among diverse topics and reinforces understanding and meaning for future applications. Students can apply their newly gained knowledge to answer questions they have about why things happen in their world and to discuss social implications.

The integration of subject areas often reveals interdependency among the disciplines. For example, both mathematics and science are required to calculate the number of calories from fat eaten in a week and find daily caloric averages. Integrating subject areas also increases the chances of stimulating student motivation by connecting to an area of interest. An example of this might be connecting physics with physical education or sports, mathematics with music, literature with history, or botany with fine arts.

> Interconnections among the academic disciplines . . . support learning by making the mathematics curriculum more meaningful.

Implications to Think About

Integrating curricula in the classroom comes in many forms. Curriculum integration may be designed and implemented by an individual classroom teacher or created by a collaborative team effort. Integrated or thematic units can be taught individually or by a multidisciplinary team of teachers, coordinating topics among otherwise separate departments. School culture often determines the most practical method for subject integration.

Mathematics can be effectively integrated at all grade levels with science, language arts, social studies, physical education, and fine arts, among other areas. Language arts (reading, writing, and communication) should be a strong component of all the disciplines. If the content is rigorous and relevant, debates, storytelling, art, music, drama, games, mnemonics, graphic organizers, and hands-on and "minds-on" laboratories can dramatically enhance student learning.

Mathematics and science are natural partners, sharing similar goals of building process and problem-solving skills. When integrated, mathematics and science provide innovative projects that encourage students to learn. For example, asking students to build a weight-bearing bridge requires them to budget, do a cost analysis of their project, and conceptualize and communicate how their completed project will look before building it.

Mathematics and social studies can be integrated in many ways. History often revolves around great advances in mathematics, and a study of important mathematical ideas helps students understand mathematical concepts and see how ideas change over time. Both societal and mathematical perspectives can provide learning opportunities.

The challenges to subject integration are lack of imagination, inadequate teacher training, hindrances to teacher collaboration, and insufficient materials. However, the benefits to the learning process should spur teachers beyond those limitations to develop quality, integrated curricula.

Resources for Learning More

American Association for the Advancement of Science. (1993). *Benchmarks for science literacy.*

Bailey, T. (1998). "Integrating vocational and academic education."

Dewey, J. (1938). *Experience and education.*

Hoachlander, G. (1997). "Organizing mathematics education around work."

Horton, R. M., Hedetniemi, T., Wiegert, E., & Wagner, J. R. (2006, April). "Integrating curriculum through themes."

O'Donnell, B. D. (2001, April). "A personal journey: Integrating mathematics and service learning."

Seki, J. M., & Menon, R. (2007, February). "Incorporating mathematics into the science program of students labeled 'at-risk.'"

Sousa, D. A. (2005). *How the brain learns.*

Urquhart, V. (2009). *Using writing in mathematics to deepen student learning.*

Vierling, L., Frykholm, J., & Glasson, G. (2006, May). "Learning mathematics and earth system science . . . via satellite."

Westwater, A., & Wolfe, P. (2000, November). "The brain-compatible curriculum."

4

How does integrated mathematics instruction affect teaching and learning?

Research and Ideas to Know About

NCTM's Learning Principle urges that classrooms be places where students regularly "engage in tasks and experiences designed to deepen and connect their knowledge" (2000, p. 21). Teachers facilitate the development of these connections when they integrate content and instruction.

When mathematics is taught in rich and realistic contexts, rather than on a purely abstract basis, more students are able to build deep understanding. Conclusions from cognitive science indicate that knowledge taught in multiple contexts better supports permanent, functional learning of concepts. Students grow in understanding when provided with rich, demanding problems that build on—rather than simply repeat—previous learning. International studies indicate that teachers in successful classrooms orchestrate learning by providing new problems to which students apply prior learning. Students who learn mathematics through complex problems and projects outperform other students whose learning is more compartmentalized and abstract. Particularly, they successfully apply relevant previous learning to new problem situations, incorporating common sense and confidence with their mathematics skills to reach a solution.

Business and industry require workers who can think and solve problems and who have integrated their knowledge. School experiences need to help build this integration. Real problems do not come neatly divided into mathematics strands. Often they require collecting real data (statistics and measurements), representing it visually (such as with coordinate geometry), and then determining an equation that closely approximates the shape of the data (algebra) in order to predict future values for the situation (probability).

Through classrooms that provide rich problem-solving situations as a way to learn mathematics, students develop a flexible understanding of the discipline and learn to integrate content and process strands of mathematics. They learn when, how, and why to use their knowledge to solve unfamiliar problems.

> When mathematics is taught in rich and realistic contexts . . . more students are able to build deep understanding.

Implications to Think About

Integrating the various branches of mathematics not only makes sense, it also saves time. Time is always a factor in student learning, and for students to build understanding, topics must be addressed with sufficient depth. The key may be to teach related topics together.

A variety of mathematics programs supporting integrated instruction are available for all grade levels. Each uses challenging contextual problems to develop understanding of important mathematics. Past programs often have not helped students make connections within mathematics or with other subjects. At the elementary level, though text materials usually contain chapters on various mathematics strands, each is isolated. Meanwhile, the conclusions of cognitive science indicate the importance of making connections in order to transfer learning.

Teachers new to integrated mathematics might learn by using problems from these programs and by observing their students. They might also examine the growing number of achievement studies of students in integrated programs.

Here are some considerations regarding an integrated approach to mathematics instruction:

- Engagement does not guarantee learning. Students can be interested without learning new mathematics.

- Allowing students to struggle enhances learning. Students need to struggle with a problem they do not know how to solve but to which they can apply known mathematics.

- True integration is not obvious by casual observation. An assortment of topics in a program does not necessarily indicate that the content is integrated. A teacher must understand, and teach, how ideas connect and are built on one another.

One important role for a mathematics teacher is to select rich, integrated mathematical tasks and problems that are accessible for all students, yet challenging enough to help them grow in mathematical understanding.

Resources for Learning More

Boaler, J. (1997). *Experiencing school mathematics: Teaching styles, sex, and setting.*

Bransford, J. D., Brown, A. L., Cocking, R. R., Donovan, M. S., & Pellegrino, J. W. (Eds.). (2000). *How people learn: Brain, mind, experience, and school.*

Dogan-Dunlap, H. (2004, January). *Changing students' perception of mathematics through an integrated, collaborative, field-based approach to teaching and learning mathematics.*

Froelich, G. W., Bartkovich, K. G., & Foerster, P. A. (1991). *Connecting mathematics: Curriculum and evaluation standards for school mathematics addenda series, grades 9–12.*

Hiebert, J. (1999, January). "Relationships between research and the NCTM standards: An introduction."

Hiebert, J., Carpenter, T. P., Fennema, E., Fuson, K. C., Wearne, D., Murray, H., et al. (1997). *Making sense: Teaching and learning mathematics with understanding.*

National Council of Teachers of Mathematics. (2000). *Principles and standards for school mathematics.*

Stigler, J. W., & Hiebert, J. (1999). *The teaching gap: Best ideas from the world's teachers for improving education in the classroom.*

Trammel, B. (2001). *Integrated mathematics? Yes, but teachers need support!*

4

How does classroom curriculum connect to the outside world?

Research and Ideas to Know About

Children learn both inside and outside the classroom. Mathematics teachers must connect these two realms of knowledge and use the connections to augment understanding of both worlds. Real life is a rich source of mathematics problems. Learning is highly interactive as students explore problems, formulate ideas, and check those ideas with peers and with their teacher through discussion and collaboration. Students build new understanding as they recognize the connections between previous learning, intuition, formalized structures, mathematical strands, and other disciplines. Students create mathematical tools and aids—symbols, schemas, and visual models—during the learning process to move from concrete reality to more abstract, higher-level thinking skills.

School mathematics has shifted away from a fixed body of knowledge calling for the mechanistic manipulation of numbers, symbols, and geometric proofs. Today, learning mathematics involves discovering why techniques work, investigating multiple approaches to problem solving, and justifying solutions.

Questions teachers should ask when selecting tasks that help connect the classroom to the outside world include the following:

- Do the tasks build on prior knowledge, proceed from informal ideas to more formal understanding, increase in complexity, or connect to other mathematics domain strands and to other disciplines?

- Do they lead to model construction, evaluation, and revision?

- Do they lead to inquiry and justification? Is the student asked to make conjectures, formulate a solution plan, solve problems, and justify their conclusion?

- Do they lead students to question themselves, question others, do research, and evaluate and reevaluate?

- Are the tasks relevant to students? Do they inspire intrinsic motivation? Do they foster personal ownership? Do they allow for unique approaches based on an individual's own knowledge? Are they challenging enough to be engaging, but not so challenging that they produce too much cognitive conflict?

> "We should all learn mathematics because it is useful, beautiful, and fun. . . . Teachers of mathematics are obliged, I believe, to do everything in their power to help their students experience the joy of mathematics."
>
> —Willoughby, 2000, pp. 10–11

Implications to Think About

Mathematics teachers need to know mathematics content, mathematics pedagogy, and how their students understand mathematical concepts. To design an appropriate curriculum, teachers need to know their students and their students' families, as well as their activities and interests.

Teachers need to understand and use the "big ideas" of mathematics—that is, ideas central to the learning of mathematics that link mathematical understandings into a coherent whole. Teachers should consistently connect new ideas to these big ideas and reinforce them throughout their instruction.

Teachers must be familiar with their students' mathematical strengths, misconceptions, favorite problem-solving approaches, and readiness to use mathematical tools. Because engaging mathematics capitalizes on realistic settings, the context of investigations is important. For instance, if students work problems that ask them to cut pizzas for fair sharing, the rational number concepts associated with such divisions will be more memorable. When problems connect to the real world, learning becomes meaningful.

Textbook companies continue to develop materials that support standards-based mathematics teaching through curriculum design that connects students to the world outside the classroom. Students frequently ask teachers the all too familiar questions: Do I really need to learn this? Will it help my future? Will I ever use it again? To answer these, teachers need to understand how mathematics concepts are used in the workforce. Car manufacturers need to be able to read blueprints (Cartesian and polar coordinates), X-ray technicians process and analyze film (data interpretation, ratios, and scale factor), and construction contractors must be able to plan and pour a level foundation (angles and geometric figures, powers, and square roots). Chefs use proportions, weights, and measures. If teachers are well versed in the mathematics found in the outside world, they can make better connections to the classroom curriculum for their students.

Resources for Learning More

Achieve. (2009). *Math works.*

Charles, R. I. (2005, Summer). "Big ideas and understandings as the foundation for elementary and middle school mathematics."

Keleher, L. A. (2006, November). "Building a career mathematics file: Challenging students to find the importance of mathematics in a variety of occupations."

Ma, L. (1999). *Knowing and teaching elementary mathematics: Teachers' understanding of fundamental mathematics in China and the United States.*

Martin, T. S. (Ed.). (2007). *Mathematics teaching today: Improving practice, improving student learning.*

National Council of Teachers of Mathematics. (1989). *Curriculum and evaluation standards for school mathematics.*

National Council of Teachers of Mathematics. (2000). *Principles and standards for school mathematics.*

Romberg, T. A., & Kaput, J. J. (1999). "Mathematics worth teaching, mathematics worth understanding."

Willoughby, S. S. (2000). "Perspectives on mathematics education."

4

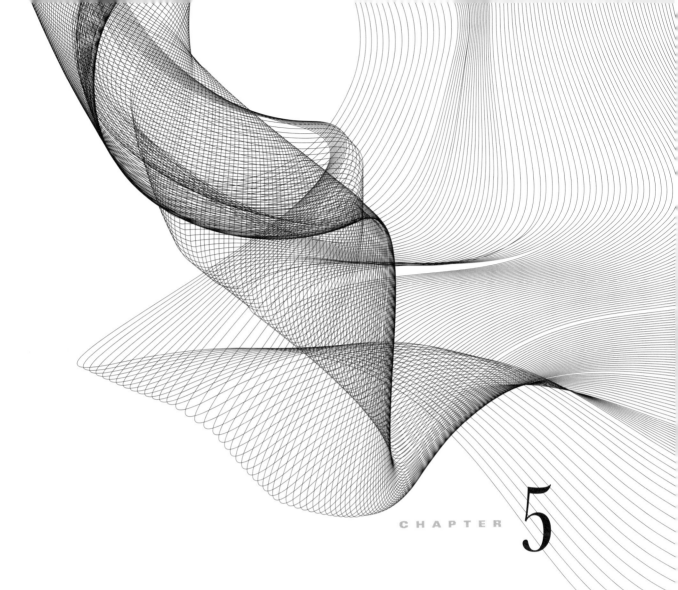

CHAPTER 5

Instructional Technology in Mathematics

Instructional technology refers to the tools used to promote classroom learning. In mathematics teaching, instructional technology is often used in problem solving, thereby making the learning experience more learner-centered. Specific technologies include various types of hardware—calculators, handheld data-collection devices, and computers—embedded software, and the Internet.

Instructional technologies such as those found in *Using Technology With Classroom Instruction That Works* add relevancy and increase student engagement. Further benefits for mathematics instruction include increased accuracy and speed in data collection and graphing; real-time visualization; interactive modeling of ambiguous mathematical processes; ability to collect, compute, and analyze large volumes of data; collaboration for data collection and interpretation; and greater opportunity to vary the presentation of results. Technology can make mathematics more meaningful and standards more attainable for all students. The Technology Principle from the *Principles and Standards for School Mathematics* states that "technology should be used widely and responsibly, with the goal of enriching students' learning of mathematics" (2000, p. 25). Technology has become ubiquitous in everyday life, and its use in the classroom enhances real-world connections and relevance.

How can using instructional technology affect mathematics reasoning and problem solving?

Research and Ideas to Know About

The education process should take advantage of the many available technologies just as mathematicians have. Whether used to construct a bisector of an angle with a straightedge and compass or to design a bridge using CAD (computer-aided design) programs, technology tools are an important part of mathematics. Technology allows us to teach traditional topics in new ways as well as teach new topics accessible only with technology. Computer-aided instruction continues to grow, and programs now include complex problem-solving software that permits students to address problems individually when multiple problems are presented simultaneously. Students can try things out, see the consequences, and then refine their thinking, thereby constructing their own knowledge. Many of these programs are in a gaming format that incorporates continual feedback mechanisms and differentiation to readily engage students. Although current research is insufficient to conclusively state the effect of instructional software, the final report of the National Mathematics Advisory Panel indicates that when implemented appropriately, high-quality instructional software can positively affect student achievement. The panel recommends continued research on which critical features of software contribute to learning.

> Technology allows us to teach traditional topics in new ways as well as teach new topics accessible only with technology.

Online or handheld calculators permit students to check their work or attack a problem differently. Certain fraction calculators permit students to choose a common factor in order to simplify improper fractions, and graphing calculators can reduce the need to manipulate algebraic expressions or equations. Such technology can help students see the connection between algebra and analytic geometry. Studies show that students who learn in a technological environment with a related algebra curriculum perform better on standard algebra manipulations, as well as modeling and problem solving, than students without that environment.

Technologies that have historically been reserved for industry are now available for educational use. These technologies allow students to use data they have collected instead of stagnant data printed in text. Examples are sensor probes like EKG sensors and barometers that, when used with computers or graphing calculators, can obtain real-time data. The Internet also permits students to obtain real data from all over the world. Using such data sets brings mathematics to life by making it relevant to current situations. Technology increases the engagement level of hard-to-reach, struggling students, such as urban youth, in mathematics. Students using such technologies are likely to show greater persistence in solving problems and are more apt to take intellectual risks. Hence, they are more likely to become productive citizens in the global, digital information-based society of the twenty-first century.

Implications to Think About

Two concerns must be addressed when using technology: how and why to use it. Students still need to know the basic facts and most of the algorithms used in a traditional mathematics program. Using technology to better teach these fundamental tenets does not imply their irrelevance. Technology should be integrated into mathematics instruction as a modern instructional tool. The NCTM Technology Principle emphasizes that tools allow students to focus on decision making, reflection, reasoning, collaboration, and problem solving without replacing basic understanding.

Teachers must also ensure equity within their school. These technologies are not just for remedial or advanced students; they allow teachers to provide differentiated instruction to meet the needs of all students. When used properly, technology motivates students to become more interested in mathematics. A student can conjecture and explore possible solutions. Some technology tools permit students with limited physical abilities to fully participate.

Instructional technology is constantly evolving. Teachers should be flexible and creative with technology as well as knowledgeable of its use and influence on student achievement. Technological devices permit students to work independently or in teams, with the teacher as a facilitator or fellow problem solver. Current instructional technology innovations—such as competency computer-based programs, computer response systems, computer algebra systems, and dynamic geometry—allow teachers to present concepts with new and exciting methods and capture student responses in ways that allow for complex analysis and tailoring of instruction.

Teachers must invest time and effort in learning these new approaches on their own or through professional development. When teachers understand the many potential uses of instructional technology, they can assess its utility in their mathematics programs.

Resources for Learning More

The Algebra Project. (2009). *The algebra project.*

Dede, C. (2007). "Reinventing the role of information and communications technologies in education."

Mistretta, R. M. (2005). "Integrating technology into the mathematics classroom: The role of teacher preparation programs."

Moses, R. P., & Cobb, C. E., Jr. (2001). *Radical equations: Math literacy and civil rights.*

National Council of Supervisors of Mathematics. (2009). *Report summary service.*

National Council of Teachers of Mathematics. (2000). *Principles and standards for school mathematics.*

National Council of Teachers of Mathematics. (2008a, March). *The role of technology in the learning and teaching of mathematics: A position of the National Council of Teachers of Mathematics.*

National Mathematics Advisory Panel. (2008). *Foundations for success: The final report of the National Mathematics Advisory Panel.*

National Research Council. (2004). *Engaging schools: Fostering high school students' motivation to learn.*

Pitler, H., Hubbell, E. R., Kuhn, M., & Malenoski, K. (2007). *Using technology with classroom instruction that works.*

Shoshani, Y., & Hazi, R. B. (2007, March). "The use of the Internet environment for enhancing creativity."

Tomlinson, C. A. (2003). *Fulfilling the promise of the differentiated classroom: Strategies and tools for responsive teaching.*

Ysseldyke, J., & Bolt, D. M. (2007). "Effect of technology-enhanced continuous progress monitoring on math achievement."

5

What effect do calculators have on student learning?

Research and Ideas to Know About

As with any instructional tool, the lesson's learning goal should determine whether using a calculator is appropriate.

After students master the underlying concepts of calculations, they can use calculators to expand their abilities. Calculators play a larger role than simply replacing paper-and-pencil computation. By efficiently processing lower-level calculations, calculators allow students to analyze, synthesize, and create larger mathematical concepts. Potential uses include developing number sense, exploring mathematical concepts such as geometry, representing and graphing data, and solving complex problems.

Although researchers have only minimally explored the use of calculators in the mathematics classroom, some findings suggest that when calculators are used in a variety of ways, students perform as well as, if not better than, those who use paper-and-pencil methods. Internationally, as students' in-class calculator use has increased, so has their level of performance on mathematics assessments. However, the final report of the National Mathematics Advisory Panel cautions that overuse of calculators may impede the development of automaticity and fluency in computation. The report states that this was a particular concern from the survey of Algebra 1 teachers. As with any instructional tool, the lesson's learning goal should determine whether using a calculator is appropriate. If the learning goal is fluency with whole-number computation, using a calculator may not be suitable. However, if the learning goal involves more complex problem solving, the calculator may be a valuable tool to promote mathematical reasoning.

Students using calculators:

- Have higher math achievement than noncalculator users, even when they can choose any tool desired

- Do better on mental computation than noncalculator users

- Experience more varied concepts and computations

- Have improved attitudes toward mathematics

- Do not become overly reliant on calculators when doing complex problem solving

Computing technologies enhance both the teaching and learning of mathematics when they are used to enable student exploration and to promote generalizations. Furthermore, studies indicate that gender differences disappear on student performance when students use graphing calculators.

Implications to Think About

Teachers can use the advantages of calculators, such as speed, to enhance student learning. Extra time allows students to try different approaches to problem solving. In the same amount of time that it takes to complete a single simple problem with the paper-and-pencil method, students can work multiple or more difficult problems using a calculator. Calculators allow students to move at their own pace and concentrate on the mathematics of problem solving rather than on computation; for instance, students who are not computationally competent can still solve intellectually challenging problems.

The use of online or handheld graphing calculators can also enhance inquiry learning by prompting more student discussions. Teachers can become classroom facilitators while students investigate mathematical concepts such as slope of a line or matrix multiplication.

Teachers can capitalize on the appropriate use of this technology to expand students' mathematical reasoning, not to replace it. Mathematical problem solving can be enhanced by calculator use because students:

- Feel more confident in initiating problem solving

- Do more exploration

- Focus more on the problem to be solved and less on the algorithm for solving

- Explain their strategies through deductive reasoning more consistently and interpret answers more readily

- Can solve more complex problems even if they are weak in basic facts

Using calculators in carefully planned ways can result in increased student problem-solving ability and improved affective outcomes without a loss of basic skills. Students need to learn the capabilities of the various technologies, including calculators. Knowing what each tool can do allows students to determine which tool to select for which purpose—and whether to use a tool at all. A skillful teacher knows how to help students develop these abilities in a balanced program focusing on mathematical thinking, fluency, and understanding.

Resources for Learning More

Cawelti, G. (Ed.). (2004). *Handbook of research on improving student achievement.*

Groves, S., & Stacey, K. (1998). "Calculators in primary mathematics: Exploring number before teaching algorithms."

Hembree, R., & Dessart, D. J. (1986, March). "Effects of hand-held calculators in precollege mathematics education: A meta-analysis."

Johnson, J. (2000). *Teaching and learning mathematics: Using research to shift from the "yesterday" mind to the "tomorrow" mind.*

Leinhardt, G., Zaslavsky, O., & Stein, M. K. (1990, Spring). "Functions, graphs, and graphing: Tasks, learning, and teaching."

Moschkovich, J., Schoenfeld, A. H., & Arcavi, A. (1993). "Aspects of understanding: On multiple perspectives and representations of linear relations and connections among them."

National Council of Teachers of Mathematics. (2005, May). *Computation, calculators, and common sense: A position of the National Council of Teachers of Mathematics.*

National Mathematics Advisory Panel. (2008). *Foundations for success: The final report of the National Mathematics Advisory Panel.*

5

How does technology affect the mathematics classroom's learning environment?

Research and Ideas to Know About

Integrating technology into instruction tends to move classrooms toward an environment in which students work cooperatively, make choices more often, and more actively take part in their learning. Instructional technology empowers students by improving their skills and concepts through multiple representations; enhanced visualization; increased construction of mathematics meaning; and individualized and customized diagnoses, remediation, and evaluation.

Instructional technology facilitates visualization of mathematical ideas, organization and analysis of data, and computational efficiency and accuracy. Many instructional technologies are tools for problem solving. Calculators, spreadsheets, graphing programs, function probes, "mathematical supposers" for making and checking conjectures, and programs modeling complex phenomena provide cognitive scaffolds to promote complex thinking, design, and learning. By using technological tools, students can become more motivated to learn and think critically, which leads to lasting knowledge.

Technology allows students more autonomy in practicing higher-order thinking skills and frees them to analyze, synthesize, and evaluate. For example, increased access to primary resources and large data sets broadens students' learning contexts and provides more opportunity for them to design real-world investigations. Real-world problems can make learning mathematics more exciting for students. Instructional technology allows them to communicate with working mathematicians and gather data in various environments. Students can also define problems that interest them and receive instantaneous feedback on the accuracy of their ideas.

Instructional technology broadens the learning community. When students collaborate, they share the process of constructing ideas, often reflecting on them in ways generally not seen in classrooms. Web 2.0 applications—such as video sharing, wikis, blogs, and podcasts—allow students to show projects to and collaborate with students worldwide. With technology, students can productively pursue their interests with fewer time constraints and intellectual barriers, thereby maximizing creativity, individuality, and the desire to learn.

"If you use graphing calculators, you arouse their interest. Students do not open a math book and say, 'Let me show you what I know on this page,' but they will show you what they know about a single button on a graphing calculator."

—Moses & Cobb, 2001, p. 117

Implications to Think About

When students experience mathematics integrated with technology, the learning environment changes. The teacher, as facilitator, moves throughout the classroom assisting individual children or the group as a whole. The teacher's role is to help students internalize concepts that can be derived from symbols, graphs, or other technological representations of mathematics.

Instructional technology allows students to use a variety of design strategies such as problem solving, creative and critical thinking, visual imagery, and reasoning; hands-on abilities such as measuring, drawing and sketching, working with computers, and using tools; and quality-control mechanisms, such as assessment and evaluative techniques. When students design their own learning environments, they can become skilled in the use and maintenance of technological products and systems, and can assess the appropriateness of these tools and systems.

It is not the classroom equipment itself, but how the equipment is used that makes the difference in student understanding. For example, tools such as dynamic geometry software allow students to construct mathematical knowledge rather than memorize facts and formulas. The keys to success lie in finding the appropriate points for integrating technology into mathematics and ensuring that the resources are available often enough to support student understanding and reflection.

When teachers prepare to integrate technology, they should be guided by the following planning questions:

- What knowledge will students learn?

- Which strategies will provide evidence that they have learned that knowledge?

- Which strategies will help students acquire and integrate that knowledge?

- Which strategies will help them practice, review, and apply the knowledge?

After these questions have been answered, teachers are ready to select supporting technologies.

Resources for Learning More

Bransford, J. D., Brown, A. L., Cocking, R. R., Donovan, M. S., & Pellegrino, J. W. (Eds.). (2000). *How people learn: Brain, mind, experience, and school.*

Burke, M. J., & Curcio, F. R. (Eds.). (2000). *Learning mathematics for a new century: 2000 yearbook.*

Cuoco, A. A. (Ed.). (2001). *The roles of representation in school mathematics: 2001 yearbook.*

Friedman, M. I., Harwell, D. H., & Schnepel, K. C. (2006). *Effective instruction: A handbook of evidence-based strategies.*

International Society for Technology in Education. (2007). *National educational technology standards for students.*

International Technology Education Association. (2000). *Standards for technological literacy: Content for the study of technology.*

Moses, R. P., & Cobb, C. E., Jr. (2001). *Radical equations: Math literacy and civil rights.*

Pitler, H., Hubbell, E. R., Kuhn, M., & Malenoski, K. (2007). *Using technology with classroom instruction that works.*

van 't Hooft, M., & Swan, K. (Eds.). (2006). *Ubiquitous computing in education: Invisible technology, visible impact.*

5

How can students best use information and data from the Internet and Web 2.0 applications?

The NCTM Technology Principle emphasizes that instructional technology tools allow students to focus on decision making, reflection, reasoning, and problem solving, and to enhance basic understanding. Many of these tools are freely available on the Internet. Students can use the Internet to access any learning resource at any time from any place. However, realizing that information on the Internet is only as good as its source, students should spend time learning how to evaluate and select reputable, usable information.

The Internet accesses current real-world data and thus provides mathematics teachers and students with an enriching resource that a textbook cannot duplicate.

Many Internet resources are available to help students embrace collaborative learning. Web 2.0, or the read/write Web, has opened up a whole new world for students to collaborate, share, and get feedback on their work. Math blogs are webpages used by teachers to organize their classes and provide discussion forums for reflection, e-portfolios, peer critiques, and project-based learning. Wikis are collaboratively built "living webpages" used by students for team projects and by teachers for math curriculum mapping. Podcasts allow students to review a class lesson or to make their own commentary on mathematics topics. Social bookmarking services let students and teachers share trusted e-resources; social media in general provide platforms for sharing images and videos and allow teachers to collaborate with other professionals with common interests anywhere in the world.

The Internet accesses current real-world data and thus provides mathematics teachers and students with an enriching resource that a textbook cannot duplicate. For instance, working on a problem in the news that involves physics, engineering, or computer science can spark student interest and may relate to what is being studied in other classes. Real data answer the question, what is this good for? Population figures, acid rain amounts, or the latest medical breakthroughs are data that teachers can use in mathematics classroom activities.

Real-world data tend to be messier than data sets supplied in textbooks; no longer does the data set for a particular problem have to result in integral solutions. Computer software and sophisticated online calculators allow students access to problem-solving methods using real data. Technology permits them to ask and try to answer their own questions generated by the data.

Implications to Think About

Students live in the information age. They read and hear of happenings around the world that interest them. Teachers can take advantage of this interest by using data from the Internet to provide the context for mathematics lessons. Furthermore, they can leverage the power of Web 2.0 applications to manipulate this data in new and engaging ways.

By looking at population-growth patterns in various states or countries, students can graph the data and predict the size of future generations. Middle school students might estimate the slopes of lines or curves and discuss interpretations, whereas high school students might use their technologies to find regression lines of best fit.

In addition to taking data from websites, students might communicate with others about data and related mathematical procedures. Presenting data and the conclusions reached from that data does not come easily, and students benefit from multiple opportunities to practice. Students can exchange data and share calculations, interpretations, and reports on various topics, such as weather or voter preferences.

Students can also sharpen their research skills by using search engines and website evaluation tools. Teachers should carefully screen Internet sites before students evaluate source credibility and determine the data's usefulness. Some sites contain data sets that may be too extensive, too complex, or in an inaccessible format for the intended instructional purpose. Although evaluation of sources is initially a teacher responsibility, students should also learn how to recognize legitimate websites that report accurate data.

Before and during the use of Web 2.0 applications, students should be taught proper online etiquette and safety precautions, such as never posting their contact information or full name and reporting any inappropriate contacts with strangers. Many online applications have built-in safety and privacy features. Teachers should familiarize themselves with these features and use them to keep the learning environment safe and honest without stifling student access and creativity.

Resources for Learning More

Beck, S. (2009). *The good, the bad and the ugly: Or, why it's a good idea to evaluate web sources.*

Frand, J. L. (2000, September/October). "The information-age mindset: Changes in students and implications for higher education."

International Society for Technology in Education. (2007). *National education technology standards for students.*

Land, S. M., & Greene, B. A. (2000). "Project-based learning with the world wide web: A qualitative study of resource integration."

National Council of Teachers of Mathematics. (2000). *Principles and standards for school mathematics.*

Pitler, H., Hubbell, E. R., Kuhn, M., & Malenoski, K. (2007). *Using technology with classroom instruction that works.*

Roempler, K. S. (2002, July). "Search smarter."

Schrock, K. (2009). *Kathy Schrock's guide for educators.*

5

How has technology changed the mathematics that is important for students to learn?

Research and Ideas to Know About

Through instructional technology, students and teachers are better able to engage in meaningful and challenging mathematical tasks.

Most mathematics teachers understand that the use of classroom technology strongly affects how mathematics is taught. Its use also influences the content and order of the mathematics curriculum. Some topics become more important because effective use of technology requires their understanding. For instance, with spreadsheets, students need a strong understanding of number sense, rounding, establishment of range and domain, and communication. Other topics become less important because the use of calculator and computer technology replaces them. These include multidigit computation, complicated factoring, and hand-drawn complex graphs. Technology allows new mathematics content to be added to the curriculum as well because it provides easy access to the necessary data, including several topics that relate to the world of work, such as large matrices, continuous compounding of interest, and creation and interpretation of fractals and statistics.

To be effective in the twenty-first century, students will need to have mathematical proficiency (that is, conceptual understanding, procedural fluency, strategic competence, adaptive reasoning, and productive disposition) to work in the fields we have yet to discover. Creativity, innovation, critical thinking, problem solving, communication, and collaboration are increasingly being recognized as skills that separate students who are prepared to live and work in the twenty-first century from those who are not.

Achievement in higher-order thinking skills is positively related to the use of technology. Technology allows students to observe mathematically accurate patterns and to form conjectures. Students' problem-solving techniques and deductive reasoning skills grow stronger because they can seek answers to their own what-if questions.

Online and handheld calculators, dynamic software, and computer simulations are a few technology tools that permit investigation of the relationships within and between mathematical topics. By using such tools, students make connections among various mathematical ideas while efficiently exploring relationships.

Implications to Think About

Using instructional technologies in the mathematics classroom not only increases the types of content that can be taught, but may also decrease the utility of some traditional content. Decisions about what is or is not obsolete mathematics content must be made thoughtfully; they should not only recognize what technology can do, but should also analyze carefully what students need to be able to do and how they need to be able to reason. The curriculum must still be about the mathematics, not about the technology. The most important instructional decision is how the technology fits with the purpose of the lesson.

The choice of problems posed in the mathematics classroom is critical to learning. Technology changes the pool of potential problems and the ways to present them. Mathematics teachers incorporating technology into the curriculum should:

- Create a vision for the best use of technology in classrooms

- Choose technologies that support established learning goals

- Determine whether a selected technology interferes with the development of a needed skill or promotes the students' ability to think independently of the technology

- Provide resources to help students gain power and fluency with technological tools

- Adapt technology for individual student needs

Technology offers teachers the opportunity to differentiate instruction and change their classrooms into dynamic learning environments. Teachers no longer have to "teach to the middle," because sophisticated software can adjust to each student's progress and keep him or her challenged yet engaged in learning.

Through instructional technology, students and teachers are better able to engage in meaningful and challenging mathematical tasks. NCLB specifically identifies technology as one way to enhance education. Administrators must ensure current use and practice for integrating technology in mathematics instruction by providing adequate and ongoing support through high-quality professional development.

Resources for Learning More

Brown, J. S., Collins, A., & Duguid, P. (1989, January). "Situated cognition and the culture of learning."

Groves, S., & Stacey, K. (1998). "Calculators in primary mathematics: Exploring number before teaching algorithms."

Johnson, J. (2000). *Teaching and learning mathematics: Using research to shift from the "yesterday" mind to the "tomorrow" mind.*

Kleiman, G. M. (2004). *What does the research say? Does technology combined with inquiry-based lessons increase students' learning?*

Lawrenz, F., Gravely, A., & Ooms, A. (2006, March). "Perceived helpfulness and amount of use of technology in science and mathematics classes at different grade levels."

North Central Regional Educational Laboratory. (2005). *Critical issue: Using technology to improve student achievement.*

Ogle, T., Branch, M., Canada, B., Christmas, O., Clement, J., Fillion, J., et al. (2002). *Technology in schools: Suggestions, tools and guidelines for assessing technology in elementary and secondary education.*

Pitler, H., Hubbell, E. R., Kuhn, M., & Malenoski, K. (2007). *Using technology with classroom instruction that works.*

Schmidt, M. E., & Vandewater, E. A. (2008, Spring). "Media and attention, cognition, and school achievement."

5

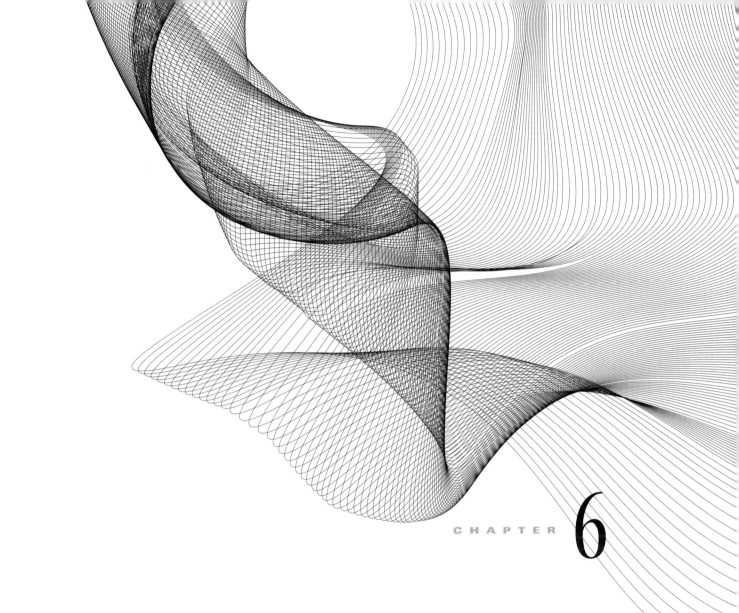

CHAPTER 6

Learning Mathematics

What does it mean to learn mathematics? This question is addressed in the *Principles and Standards for School Mathematics*. Children are natural learners. They are inquisitive about patterns and shapes, recognizing and creating them from a young age. They count, measure, and share objects. For children, mathematics is learned by doing. Their school experience of mathematics learning should include problem solving and reasoning through grade 12, not simply lectures, books, and worksheets.

During the twentieth century, educators' understanding of the learning process progressed from behavioral observations through cognitive psychology to improved knowledge about neurophysiology. The 1990s were dubbed "the decade of the brain" because of the tremendous increase in understanding of how the brain works. Twenty-first-century educators are improving their classroom practice through application of the newest understandings from neuroscience.

How can we promote the importance of learning mathematics to the public?

Research and Ideas to Know About

Since the 1990s the general public has become more aware of mathematics education reform than ever before. Publications such as the National Commission on Excellence in Education's *A Nation at Risk*, the standards-setting work of the National Council of Teachers of Mathematics, and reports from TIMSS, PISA, and the National Mathematics Advisory Panel highlight the need for reform. Most people agree that mathematical literacy extends beyond knowledge of mathematics concepts and procedures into the ability to create mathematical models of situations, solve the problems represented by the models, and interpret the solutions in terms of societal implications.

Today students who graduate with weak math skills will not be able to compete in the evolving global economy and job market.

The National Commission on Mathematics and Science Teaching report *Before It's Too Late* cites four compelling reasons students should become competent in mathematics and science: (1) the pace of change in the global economy and the American workplace, (2) the need for both mathematics and science in everyday decision making, (3) national security interests, and (4) the intrinsic value of mathematics and science to society. According to the National Science Board, jobs related to science, technology, engineering, and mathematics (STEM) are outpacing overall job growth by three to one. The United States does not have enough qualified domestic candidates to fill these jobs. With the anticipated growth in STEM jobs, promoting student interest in these fields is a national interest.

The value of learning mathematics today is evident in America's need to stay globally competitive. Today, students who graduate with weak math skills will not be able to compete in the evolving global economy and job market. The Organisation for Economic Co-operation and Development found that the United States is failing to produce enough science and engineering graduates. The number of four-year-college science graduates per 100,000 employed twenty-five- to thirty-four-year-olds is 195 less than other developed nations and between 400 and 1,100 less than Austria, the United Kingdom, and Korea. Students who take advanced mathematics courses in high school perform significantly better in college science courses. In 2008, economists estimated that if the United States improved its mathematics and science achievement to become globally competitive, the U.S. gross domestic product could eventually grow by an additional 36 percent.

Implications to Think About

Mathematical literacy is the goal for all students, not just for those preparing for college or for a career dependent on higher-level mathematics. Mathematical literacy includes using mathematics-related knowledge on a personal and societal level, addressing issues by asking questions, using evidence to propose explanations or answers, and becoming informed citizens. Learning expectations must be high for all students. To promote the goal of mathematics literacy and the vision of quality mathematics education, the entire preK–12 educational system must be aligned and must focus on providing:

- Important content in solid mathematics curricula

- Competent and knowledgeable mathematics teachers who can integrate instruction and assessment

- Education policies that support and enhance learning

- Connections across disciplines

- Mathematics classrooms with access to technology

- Preparation for future careers

- Tools and strategies to assist decision making on mathematics-based issues

To offer high-quality, preK–12 mathematics learning experiences for all students, content-qualified instructors must teach consistent and coherent programs. Administrators can offer positive support by providing access to mathematics resources, ensuring that a competent mathematics teacher is in every classroom, and promoting ongoing opportunities for high-quality professional development. A principal message in the final report of the National Mathematics Advisory Panel cites the central role of knowledgeable mathematics teachers in mathematics education and encourages citizens and leadership to seek initiatives for recruiting, preparing, evaluating, and retaining effective teachers.

Outreach by mathematics educators to parents and the school community can help achieve a shared commitment to improve mathematics education. Because parental attitudes about mathematics predict student success, parents must help teachers guide students to understand the critical need to learn mathematics.

Resources for Learning More

Achieve. (2009). *Math works.*

Campbell, P. B. (1992). *Math, science, and your daughter: What can parents do?*

Mirra, A. (2003). *Administrator's guide: How to support and improve mathematics education in your school.*

Mirra, A. (Ed.). (2005). *A family's guide: Fostering your child's success in school mathematics.*

National Commission on Excellence in Education. (1983). *A nation at risk: The imperative for educational reform.*

National Commission on Mathematics and Science Teaching for the 21st Century. (2000). *Before it's too late: A report to the nation from the National Commission on Mathematics and Science Teaching for the 21st Century.*

National Council of Teachers of Mathematics. (2000). *Principles and standards for school mathematics.*

National Mathematics Advisory Panel. (2008). *Foundations for success: The final report of the National Mathematics Advisory Panel.*

National Research Council. (1989). *Everybody counts: A report to the nation on the future of mathematics education.*

National Science Board. (2008). *Science and engineering indicators 2008.*

Organisation for Economic Co-operation and Development. (2007). *Education at a glance.*

Organisation for Economic Co-operation and Development. (2008). *OECD science, technology and industry outlook.*

6

What do we know about how students learn mathematics?

Research and Ideas to Know About

Today's educators have a greater understanding of how students learn mathematics. The use of manipulatives, a focus on algebraic concepts throughout the mathematics program, problems set in meaningful contexts, and ample opportunities and time to learn are all important. Research indicates that manipulatives, in particular, can be effective in mathematics instruction. Although primary teachers generally accept the importance of manipulatives, some studies of student mathematics learning have created interest in using manipulatives across all grades. It is important, however, to keep the focus on mathematics, because otherwise students may learn only about the manipulative and miss the mathematics content.

Teachers must carefully choose activities and manipulatives that effectively support the introduction of abstract symbols. A principal message of the final report of the National Mathematics Advisory Panel calls for using instructional practices and strategies that are clearly known from rigorous research about how children learn.

Students may have difficulty making the transition from arithmetic to algebra, but research indicates that development of algebraic reasoning can be supported in elementary and middle school. Young students can learn algebraic concepts, especially algebraic representation and the notions of variable and function; the basic concepts can be introduced as patterning and as a generalization of arithmetic. For example, students can look for and analyze patterns on a hundreds chart.

Students can learn about mathematical topics best through solving meaningful, contextual problems and through collaborative mathematical discussions. Students do benefit somewhat from seeing problems solved, but they receive the most benefit from solving problems themselves and having the opportunity to explain their thinking. High-quality mathematics discussions about concepts, procedures, and problem solving help students understand more deeply and clearly. Appropriate questioning techniques by both teacher and student enhance the development of student problem-solving skills.

Students must have ample opportunities to learn if they are to fully develop their mathematical proficiency. Students need school time for regular, sustained engagement in the study of mathematics, including meaningful practice built on understanding. In addition, student practice is enhanced by timely feedback on work.

> Students must have ample opportunities to learn if they are to fully develop their mathematical proficiency.

Implications to Think About

School programs should provide rich activities involving number and operations that enable students to either build on their informal learning or to learn without prior instruction. They need to have experiences with concrete materials when learning concepts at any level, and instructional materials and classroom teaching should help students transition from the concrete to the abstract. For this to occur, teachers should select instructional materials that focus on the mathematics being taught.

Students must have a thorough understanding of the base ten and decimal place value representations as well as fluency with multidigit numbers and decimal fractions. They should experience learning activities featuring algebraic concepts beginning in early elementary. In middle school, algebraic ideas should be developed more robustly and integrated with other concepts. For example, teachers could introduce the central ideas of calculus, such as rate of change, to students throughout elementary and middle school grades.

Teachers should spend significant class time developing mathematical ideas and methods within an environment that provides rich opportunities for students to solve contextual problems in groups or individually. Classroom discussions should include mathematical connections, other solution methods, and mathematical justifications, and students should have opportunities to verbalize their thought processes and work collaboratively. Many students benefit from hearing what their peers are thinking.

Teacher questioning techniques should elicit students' thought processes and solution strategies and give students opportunities to clarify their understanding. Often, changing the form of a question from single answer to one that allows students various ways to achieve an end result will increase student creativity and motivation. For example, beyond asking students to answer items such as, "Simplify $4x + 3x$," students also could be asked questions such as, "What are four ways to represent the function $y = 7x$?" The latter question assesses student understanding while stimulating more creative thought.

Resources for Learning More

Carpenter, T. P., Levi, L., & Farnsworth, V. (2000, Fall). "Building a foundation for learning algebra in the elementary grades."

Chapin, S. H. (2003). *Classroom discussions: Using math talk to help students learn, grades 1–6.*

De Corte, E., Greer, B., & Verschaffel, L. (1996). "Mathematics teaching and learning."

Kilpatrick, J., Swafford, J., & Findell, B. (Eds.). (2001). *Adding it up: Helping children learn mathematics.*

National Mathematics Advisory Panel. (2008). *Foundations for success: The final report of the National Mathematics Advisory Panel.*

National Research Council. (2005). *How students learn: History, mathematics, and science in the classroom.*

Schwartz, S. L. (2005). *Teaching young children mathematics.*

Sousa, D. A. (2007). *How the brain learns mathematics.*

Williams, D. L. (2007, April). "The what, why, and how of contextual teaching in a mathematics classroom."

6

What does learning theory show teachers about how students learn mathematics?

Research and Ideas to Know About

A learning theory–based instructional approach offers students an opportunity to take control of their learning through a more personal connection.

Knowledge changes throughout a person's development and is culturally and socially mediated. Students are not empty vessels to be filled with knowledge; rather, they build their own knowledge structures. NCTM builds a case through its Learning Principle for going beyond rote memorization: "Students must learn mathematics with understanding, actively building new knowledge from experience and prior knowledge" (2000, p. 20). Planning courses of action, weighing alternatives, applying prior knowledge to new ways of thinking or new ideas, and making sense of the world are not only instructional strategies supported by learning theory, but also skills of informed citizenship.

The human brain searches for patterns in sensory input and memory. It analyzes complex information into component parts and synthesizes simple facts into concepts. The brain initially pays primary attention to the emotional content of information but can be focused through metacognition. Because it is changed by every act of learning, whether intentional or peripheral, each brain is unique. To apply brain research on learning, mathematics teachers should link new instruction to students' prior knowledge by employing teaching strategies that draw on varied learning styles.

Teachers' use of learning theory encourages student-centered learning environments. When teachers align instruction about facts, procedures, and concepts, they help strengthen student learning about all three. When students connect new learning to previously learned material, subsequent learning becomes easier and students are more apt to experience a sense of mathematical power.

A learning theory–based instructional approach offers students an opportunity to take control of their learning through a more personal connection, which gives greater meaning to the acquired knowledge or skill. A mathematics classroom organized to promote learning values and encourage student interaction and cooperation provides access to learning materials from realistic contexts and allows students to generate their own ways of learning.

Implications to Think About

Learning is not a passive activity. When designing mathematics instruction, educators should rely on learning theory to guide their development of effective learning experiences.

Teachers should correct any misconceptions about mathematics topics that students might have, although changing long-held concepts in light of new information can be a complex and time-consuming process. Effective teaching requires not only sound knowledge of correct mathematics information, but also knowledge of common misconceptions and how to deal with them. Without the latter, students' attempts to combine new instruction with prior misconceptions can have unanticipated learning outcomes.

Effective mathematics teachers play a pivotal role in helping students search for deeper knowledge and skill. They probe for greater justification of student-generated ideas and deeper explanations of relationships and of how mathematics works, using questions such as:

- *How does this operation work?*

- *What generalization can you make from this mathematical situation? Defend your ideas.*

- *What alternative strategy can you develop for this procedure?*

- *How can you justify your answer?*

- *What patterns or relationships apply to this problem? Describe the ones you found.*

These types of questions emphasize student-to-student interactions and justification of their ideas, while valuing their knowledge and skill. The teacher, therefore, does not dominate the material or the conversation. Instead, his or her role is to help students shape their ideas while simultaneously honing their skills.

Students of teachers who plan instruction based on learning theory are more likely to take intellectual risks. They are willing to accept challenges to their misconceptions. Students who build new learning demonstrate their understanding rather than simply repeat what they are taught. Teachers who model building mathematical knowledge and who design learning environments that support it are honoring their students as emerging mathematicians.

Resources for Learning More

Bransford, J. D., Brown, A. L., Cocking, R. R., Donovan, M. S., & Pellegrino, J. W. (Eds.). (2000). *How people learn: Brain, mind, experience, and school.*

Brooks, J. G., & Brooks, M. G. (1993). *In search of understanding: The case for constructivist classrooms.*

Caine, R. N., & Caine, G. (1994). *Making connections: Teaching and the human brain.*

Kilpatrick, J., Martin, W. G., & Schifter, D. (Eds.). (2003). *A research companion to principles and standards for school mathematics.*

National Council of Teachers of Mathematics. (2000). *Principles and standards for school mathematics.*

Phye, G. D. (Ed.). (1997). *Handbook of academic learning: Construction of knowledge.*

Ronis, D. (2006). *Brain-compatible mathematics.*

Schmidt, M. E., & Vandewater, E. A. (2008, Spring). "Media and attention, cognition, and school achievement."

Sousa, D. A. (2005). *How the brain learns.*

Steffe, L. P., & Wiegel, H. G. (1996). "On the nature of a model of mathematical learning."

6

What roles do basic skills play in mathematics instruction?

Research and Ideas to Know About

An early definition of basic mathematical skills referred only to computation, arithmetic facts, and symbol manipulation. Today, it is clearly important that students solve problems; apply mathematics in everyday situations; use logical reasoning; and have an understanding of basic concepts of algebra, geometry, measurement, statistics or data analysis, and probability. All of these topics are incorporated in the new definition of basic mathematics skills.

Many of the topics that form the new definition of basic skills are discussed in other sections of this resource, so here the focus is only on arithmetic. For example, command of addition, subtraction, multiplication, and division facts are essential in understanding computational processes. Students who commit basic facts to memory and become computationally fluent spend more time on the problem-solving process and thereby are more likely to become successful problem solvers. Automatic access to basic facts frees up a student's mental processes to allow directed focus on problem solving. The final report of the National Mathematics Advisory Panel cites fluency with whole numbers and with fractions as critical components in student readiness for algebra coursework.

It is also important to note that abundant research evidence shows that proficient calculation skills and basic facts mastery need not precede conceptual understanding and problem solving. Students find that well-chosen motivating and interesting problems help with both learning and retaining mathematical ideas. Even basic facts can be learned relatively effortlessly through meaningful repetition in the context of solving problems or playing games. When students encounter a variety of contexts and tasks, they have more opportunity to develop and use thinking strategies that support and reinforce learning facts.

As mathematics teachers increasingly use the latest calculator and computer technologies, enhanced conceptions of basic skills in arithmetic and algebra are appearing. Number sense, symbol sense, and strategies for mental computation and reasoned estimation are receiving greater emphasis. Reliance on paper-and-pencil routines for more complex calculation has diminished as students have embraced the power of technology.

"The automaticity in putting a skill to use frees up mental energy to focus on the more rigorous demands of a complicated problem."

—Wu, 1999, p. 15

Implications to Think About

Students need to learn the most efficient strategies to master basic arithmetic facts. For example, 7 + 8 can be thought of as (7 + 7) + 1, and the answer to 7 $\times$ 8 can be determined from (5 $\times$ 8) + (2 $\times$ 8), or from (7 $\times$ 7) + 7. Such strategies rely on number sense and meaningful mathematical relationships. Students learn new facts more easily when they generate new knowledge rather than rely on memorization. Derived fact strategies—strategies that help learners find the solution to unknown number facts using a small set of known number facts—improve recall and provide fall-back mechanisms for students. Facts and methods learned with understanding are connected to each other and to prior knowledge, are easier to remember and use, and can be reconstructed when forgotten. Learning with understanding is more powerful than simple memorization because the act of organizing information improves retention, promotes fluency, and facilitates learning related material.

Measurement skills that students learn in elementary school also are useful when they learn formal algebraic skills in high school. The product of the multiplication of two binomials (x + 2) and (x + 3) can be thought of as the area of a rectangle having sides with lengths (x + 2) and (x + 3). The result is one "big" square (x by x), five rectangles (1 by x), and 6 "little" squares, or $x^2 + 5x + 6$.

Procedural knowledge is best developed on a foundation of conceptual understanding. Practice toward mastery should not precede meaning. Drill does not guarantee immediate recall or contribute to growth in understanding. Practice is important, and once students understand a computation procedure, practice helps them become confident and competent in using it. But when students mimic a procedure without understanding, it is difficult for them to go back later and build understanding.

Resources for Learning More

Bass, H. (2003, February). "Computational fluency, algorithms, and mathematical proficiency: One mathematician's perspective."

Carpenter, T. P., Fennema, E., Franke, M. L., Levi, L., & Empson, S. B. (1999). *Children's mathematics: Cognitively guided instruction*.

Fuson, K. C. (1992). "Research on learning and teaching addition and subtraction of whole numbers."

Hiebert, J., & Carpenter, T. P. (1992). "Learning and teaching with understanding."

Johnson, J. (2000). *Teaching and learning mathematics: Using research to shift from the "yesterday" mind to the "tomorrow" mind.*

Kilpatrick, J., Swafford, J., & Findell, B. (Eds.). (2001). *Adding it up: Helping children learn mathematics*.

National Council of Teachers of Mathematics. (2000). *Principles and standards for school mathematics*.

National Mathematics Advisory Panel. (2008). *Foundations for success: The final report of the National Mathematics Advisory Panel*.

Wu, H. (1999, Fall). "Basic skills versus conceptual understanding: A bogus dichotomy in mathematics education."

6

What is the role of algorithms in mathematics instruction?

Algorithms and algorithmic study are important mathematical ideas that all students need to use and understand. An *algorithm* is a precise, step-by-step method or set of rules for solving a particular type of problem. Algorithmic study involves applying, developing, analyzing, and understanding the nature of algorithms. Although many types of algorithms are used in all fields of mathematics, the focus here is on those associated with arithmetic operations.

Understanding algorithms is central to developing computational fluency.

How to teach well-established (standard or conventional) arithmetic algorithms is the subject of debate, especially between traditional and reform approaches. Research foci about algorithmic development and computational fluency include the value of standard, student-invented, and alternative algorithms; the value and place of drill in learning algorithms; and the place of algorithms in a technological world.

To become fluent in calculation, students must have efficient, accurate methods supported by number and operation sense, and they must know how algorithms work. Thoughtful use of standard algorithms advances fluency. However, rote learning of these traditional paper-and-pencil algorithms can interfere with the development of number sense. Further, early introduction and practice of algorithms may legitimize a single procedure and limit students' computational fluency so that they cannot choose methods that best fit the numbers or situation. The final report of the National Mathematics Advisory Panel states that curricula must simultaneously develop conceptual understandings, computational fluency, and problem-solving skills.

Speed and efficiency in using arithmetic algorithms with large numbers is not as critical as it once was, and because of that, drilling to achieve such a goal holds little value. But many everyday mathematics tasks require facility with algorithms for computation. Technology has not rendered obsolete the need to understand and be able to perform some basic written algorithms.

Implications to Think About

Learning to use "standard" algorithms should be part of the mathematics curriculum. In addition to providing computational tools, algorithms can be important tools in their own right. They can be analyzed and compared, helping students understand the nature and properties of operations, place value concepts for numbers, and characteristics of good algorithms.

Mathematics teachers need to understand the importance of alternative algorithms. Developing and discussing invented algorithms enhances students' number and operation sense. When students record, explain, and critique one another's strategies, they learn about efficiency, validity, and generalizability. A teacher can introduce various standard algorithms or note them as they arise naturally during discussions. Students will remember and implement algorithmic procedures better if they have time to make sense of them.

Appropriate practice is connected to mathematical thinking through reasoning, communicating, and problem solving. Appropriate practice reminds students that mathematics is well structured—organized, filled with patterns, and predictable—and that the power of algorithms resides in their applicability as a tool for both routine tasks and solving mathematics problems.

Learning a traditional algorithm means learning not only how to execute it with several examples or situations, but also being able to explain its mathematical significance and prove that its various steps produce a correct answer. Understanding algorithms is central to developing computational fluency. Being able to compute fluently includes making smart choices about which tools to use and when. Students should have opportunities to choose among mental computation, paper-and-pencil algorithms, estimation, and calculator use. Ability to use algorithms enhances these choices.

Resources for Learning More

Bass, H. (2003, February). "Computational fluency, algorithms, and mathematical proficiency: One mathematician's perspective."

Carroll, W., & Porter, D. (1998). "Alternative algorithms for whole-number operations."

Hiebert, J. (1999, January). "Relationships between research and the NCTM standards: An introduction."

Johnson, J. (2000). *Teaching and learning mathematics: Using research to shift from the "yesterday" mind to the "tomorrow" mind.*

Kamii, C., & Dominick, A. (1998). "The harmful effects of algorithms in grades 1–4."

Kilpatrick, J., Swafford, J., & Findell, B. (Eds.). (2001). *Adding it up: Helping children learn mathematics.*

National Council of Teachers of Mathematics. (2000). *Principles and standards for school mathematics.*

National Mathematics Advisory Panel. (2008). *Foundations for success: The final report of the National Mathematics Advisory Panel.*

Steen, L. A. (1990). *On the shoulders of giants: New approaches to numeracy.*

6

What factors contribute most strongly to student success in learning mathematics?

Research and Ideas to Know About

One of the strongest predictors of student success is teacher quality.

One important contributing factor to student success is active participation with mathematics. Students who engage in mathematical modeling, problem solving, and reasoning apply the mathematics they are learning. Supporting practices include providing ample time to perform investigations, emphasizing discourse among students and between students and teachers, asking students to reflect on their work, allotting time to revise work, and acknowledging student diversity. The instructional practice of covering many discrete topics does not help students develop deep understanding and useful performance skills.

Teachers who set up active learning tasks that engage students in purposeful work spend substantial time moving about the classroom working with individuals and small groups. They make note of individual student accomplishments and needs, redirect students to new tasks as necessary, and listen as students reason their way through a problem. Students who experience a range of activities from short whole-group instruction to extended periods when they are engaged in problem solving are more likely to enjoy learning. A positive student-teacher relationship improves learning. In fact, research indicates that "social and intellectual support from peers and teachers is associated with higher mathematics performance for all students, and that such support is especially important for many African-American and Hispanic students" (National Mathematics Advisory Panel, 2008, p. 32).

One of the strongest predictors of student success is teacher quality; highly qualified teachers in both mathematics content knowledge and pedagogical skills are more effective. Those who continue their education while teaching tend to develop an even deeper understanding of content applications, content knowledge, effective instructional strategies, theoretical bases for instructional decisions, and confidence in decision making. In general, teachers who continue learning throughout their careers are more likely to become conscientious, competent, and professional.

Implications to Think About

The teacher's instructional decision making contributes greatly to student success in mathematics classes. Students who approach learning mathematics in realistic contexts, who work as mathematicians do, and who are held to the performance criteria of mathematicians demonstrate the best understanding of mathematical concepts.

Class scheduling is of major importance to both administrators and teachers. Administrators need to examine teacher schedules to facilitate common planning time—a professional, collegial time during which teachers design appropriate contextual problem-solving experiences for their students and cooperatively examine student work samples as a means of informing instruction. In addition, teachers must provide classroom time for the in-depth study of major concepts in mathematics. Short, segmented class periods do not support the time necessary to explore topics in-depth or from multiple perspectives and often prevent students from achieving the flow and continuity of thinking that is so critical in making sense of mathematics.

Teachers help frame key ideas from students' prior knowledge, anticipate misconceptions, and design learning experiences that build on student thinking and reflect mathematics content aligned with the *Principles and Standards for School Mathematics*. Students need to be active listeners and able to restate in their own words what others contribute. Those who are encouraged to try out new ideas, think aloud, and get specific feedback from others are more apt to internalize the mathematical concepts they are exploring. Teachers learn from watching and listening to their students, and students learn by articulating what they know. Successful mathematics students have teachers who stay current in mathematics as well as mathematics education. Effective mathematics teachers:

- Read and apply relevant research in mathematics pedagogy and education

- Keep abreast of changes in mathematics content

- Are active members of their professional mathematics education organizations

Resources for Learning More

Barber, M., & Mourshed, M. (2007). *How the world's best-performing school systems come out on top.*

Bransford, J. D., Brown, A. L., Cocking, R. R., Donovan, M. S., & Pellegrino, J. W. (Eds.). (2000). *How people learn: Brain, mind, experience, and school.*

Darling-Hammond, L. (1997). *The right to learn: A blueprint for creating schools that work.*

Hill, H. C., Rowan, B., & Loewenberg Ball, D. (2005, Summer). "Effects of teachers' mathematical knowledge for teaching on student achievement."

Kilpatrick, J., Martin, W. G., & Schifter, D. (Eds.). (2003). *A research companion to principles and standards for school mathematics.*

Meier, D. (1995). *The power of their ideas: Lessons for America from a small school in Harlem.*

National Council of Teachers of Mathematics. (2000). *Principles and standards for school mathematics.*

National Mathematics Advisory Panel. (2008). *Foundations for success: The final report of the National Mathematics Advisory Panel.*

Richard-Amato, P. A., & Snow, M. A. (Eds.). (2005). *Academic success for English language learners: Strategies for K–12 mainstream teachers.*

Stigler, J. W., & Hiebert, J. (1999). *The teaching gap: Best ideas from the world's teachers for improving education in the classroom.*

Tomlinson, C. A. (2003). *Fulfilling the promise of the differentiated classroom: Strategies and tools for responsive teaching.*

6

How do students' attitudes affect their performance and future opportunities?

Research and Ideas to Know About

Students' attitudes toward mathematics greatly influence their achievement. *Attitudes* are stable dispositions, affective responses, or beliefs individuals have that develop largely through experience. Students who enjoy mathematics tend to perform well in their coursework and are more likely to enroll in advanced mathematics courses. Conversely, students who dislike mathematics tend not to do well in these classes and/or do not attempt the more advanced mathematics classes in secondary school.

Students who enjoy mathematics tend to perform well in their coursework.

Negative attitudes about mathematics are learned, not inherited. Students enter school with a considerable amount of enthusiasm and curiosity that naturally produce mathematical questions: What is the distance between my home and school? How likely am I to win this game? Do I have enough paint to finish this project? Students have positive emotions when they make mathematical conjectures, solve problems, and see connections between important ideas. Of course, students can also experience frustration when not making progress toward solving a problem. Teachers should provide appropriately challenging problems so that students can learn and establish the norm of perseverance for successful problem solving.

Too often, mathematics instruction serves to alienate students rather than reveal to them its usefulness. A student with a productive attitude finds sense in mathematics, perceives it as useful and worthwhile, believes that steady effort in learning mathematics pays off, and views him or herself as an effective learner and doer of mathematics. Research suggests that minority students and females often learn to doubt their mathematical abilities early on and, as a consequence, are more likely to attribute failure to lack of ability. Generally, U.S. students are more likely to attribute success in mathematics problem solving to ability rather than effort. East Asian children, on the other hand, are more likely to perceive success as a function of effort, not ability. It is important for teachers to model perseverance, convey that mistakes and misconceptions are inevitable, and provide opportunities for learning. In addition, both students and teachers must believe that all students can learn mathematics.

Implications to Think About

Classroom practices, culture, and norms strongly influence student attitudes, particularly during elementary school years when students form attitudes toward school and academics. Findings suggest that among high-poverty students, an emphasis on conformity, competition, and mathematics as rules decreases motivation and achievement when compared to a more exploratory curriculum. Students are less likely to think flexibly and critically when their schools emphasize order, obedience, acceptance of school and mathematical rules, and dependence on the structures provided by these rules. While an organized learning environment is important, promoting students' comfortable exploration of mathematics through challenging open-ended problems should replace classroom norms that elevate procedures, rules, competition, and speed. However, while fostering students' positive attitudes toward mathematics, teachers need to be careful not to simplify a challenging curriculum or alleviate all frustration during problem solving.

Successful teachers communicate explicit expectations that students will adequately justify their answers, persist at problem solving when faced with frustration, and solve problems independently. Students of these teachers show satisfaction and enthusiasm for problem solving and demonstrate an autonomous view of themselves as learners. Effective mathematics teachers establish good relationships with students by being friendly rather than formal, sharing personal anecdotes that illustrate their own problem-solving strengths and weaknesses, and establishing systems that hold students accountable for their performance. Most of these teachers focus on aspects of student performance other than obtaining correct answers. These teachers also tend to use cooperative groups to promote independence and reduce students' frustration.

Fostering these desirable classroom norms with low-achieving students is equally critical. Teachers must provide all students with learning opportunities that allow them to make sense of mathematics.

Resources for Learning More

The Algebra Project. (2009). *The algebra project.*

Boaler, J. (1997). *Experiencing school mathematics: Teaching styles, sex, and setting.*

Halpern, D. F., Aronson, J., Reimer, N., Simpkins, S., Star, J. R., & Wentzel, K. (2007). *Encouraging girls in math and science.*

Henningsen, M., & Stein, M. K. (1997, November). "Mathematical tasks and student cognition: Classroom-based factors that support and inhibit high-level mathematical thinking and reasoning."

Kilpatrick, J., Swafford, J., & Findell, B. (Eds.). (2001). *Adding it up: Helping children learn mathematics.*

Lester, F. K. (Ed.). (2007). *Second handbook of research on mathematics teaching and learning.*

Morge, S. P. (2007, August). "Eliciting students' beliefs about who is good at mathematics."

Schackow, J. B., & Thompson, D. R. (2005, Fall). "High school students' attitudes toward mathematics."

Stigler, J. W., & Hiebert, J. (2004, February). "Improving mathematics teaching."

6

How can teachers help students reflect on and communicate their own learning?

Research and Ideas to Know About

Metacognition, sometimes referred to as thinking about thinking, is an excellent way to help students reflect on and communicate their learning.

Metacognitive strategies, portfolios, and structured classroom writing assignments support students' personal construction of mathematics understanding. Learning increases after explicit instruction in metacognitive strategies. Metacognitive strategies to manage thinking include:

- Connecting newly learned information with information that is already known

- Carefully choosing appropriate thinking strategies for a specific use

- Planning, monitoring, and judging the effectiveness of thinking processes

Creating and maintaining portfolios of personal work is one strategy that encourages reflection. The process of selecting and organizing the contents of a portfolio builds self-awareness. Using classroom portfolios gives students more control over their own learning. It also supports the teacher's role as a facilitator of learning.

Writing is another way for students to discover, organize, summarize, and communicate knowledge. Writing makes thinking processes concrete and increases retention of concepts. The act of writing gives students access to their thinking processes, enabling them to construct new meaningful and applicable understandings.

When students interact around the mathematics they are learning, they are better able to make connections among concepts and topics and to reorganize their knowledge. When students talk about the strategies, teachers can help them build on their informal knowledge. By facilitating classroom interactions, encouraging students to propose mathematical ideas, helping them learn to evaluate their own thinking and that of others, and developing their reasoning skills, teachers can enhance mathematics learning.

Metacognitive strategies, portfolios, and structured classroom writing assignments support students' personal construction of mathematics understanding.

Implications to Think About

Students develop metacognitive strategies through frequent challenging problem solving. Metacognitive activities in mathematics classes can ask students to:

- Identify what is known and not known (for example, K-W-L—what I know/want to know/learned)

- Talk about thinking—first through teacher modeling (think-alouds), then in group discussion, culminating in paired problem solving

- Maintain a thinking journal or learning log (such as a process diary)

- Take increased responsibility for planning activities

- Practice targeted self-regulation skills following direct instruction (for example, estimating time requirements, organizing materials, and scheduling)

- Debrief thinking processes during class closure (for example, review thinking processes, identify and classify strategies used, evaluate successes, and seek alternatives)

- Participate in guided self-evaluation

Writing tasks must be authentic—that is, the text must address a real audience, sometimes oneself. Students can use their journals to reflect on knowledge, feelings, and beliefs. Journals can open a dialogue between learner and teacher that leads to more individualized instruction and support. Throughout the year, topics for journal writing should start with affective, open-ended prompts (*Describe a time when you felt successful in solving a mathematical problem. Why did you feel that way?*), proceed to review of familiar mathematics concepts (*How did you determine the line of symmetry?*), and move toward discussion of more advanced mathematics concepts that extend and reinforce new understanding.

Other useful writing assignments include analytic essays—which develop links between concepts—and concept maps or hierarchical outlines—which can facilitate meaningful cooperative learning, identify misconceptions, evaluate understanding, and demonstrate construction of mathematical knowledge.

Resources for Learning More

Blakey, E., & Spence, S. (1990). *Developing metacognition.*

Bransford, J. D., Brown, A. L., Cocking, R. R., Donovan, M. S., & Pellegrino, J. W. (Eds.). (2000). *How people learn: Brain, mind, experience, and school.*

Foster, G., Sawicki, E., Schaeffer, H., & Zelinski, V. (2002). *I think, therefore I learn!*

Goldberg, P. D., & Bush, W. S. (2003, Fall). "Using metacognitive skills to improve 3rd graders' math problem solving."

Lester, F. K. (Ed.). (2007). *Second handbook of research on mathematics teaching and learning.*

Martin, T. S. (Ed.). (2007). *Mathematics teaching today: Improving practice, improving student learning.*

National Council of Teachers of Mathematics. (2000). *Principles and standards for school mathematics.*

Pugalee, D. K. (2004, March). "A comparison of verbal and written descriptions of students' problem solving processes."

Urquhart, V., & McIver, M. (2005). *Teaching writing in the content areas.*

Wisconsin Department of Public Instruction. (2007). *Adolescent learning toolkit.*

Wolfe, P. (2001). *Brain matters: Translating research into classroom practice.*

6

What role does active, hands-on learning play in mathematics instruction?

Research and Ideas to Know About

Mathematical learning in young children is strongly linked to sense perception and concrete experience. Children move toward an understanding of symbols, and eventually abstract concepts, only after they experience concrete ideas.

When students can touch and move objects to make visual representations of mathematical concepts, different learning modalities are addressed.

Mathematics achievement is increased through the long-term use of concrete instructional materials and active lessons at various grade levels. The more avenues there are available to receive data through the senses, the more connections the brain can make, and the better a learner can understand a new idea. This holds not only for primary age–learners, but also through adulthood. All students need to learn mathematics by actively doing mathematics through activities such as physically measuring objects, collecting and representing data, and handling geometric solids from the earliest ages. Other active learning experiences include representing groups of ten with locking cubes, sorting mathematical objects or cards picturing shapes, or using tiles to represent algebraic quantities. The National Library of Virtual Manipulatives offers free access to an interactive web-based tool for further student engagement. Students also enjoy acting out problems or equations.

Students do not discover or understand mathematical concepts solely by manipulating concrete materials. Teachers must intervene frequently to help students focus on underlying mathematical ideas and to build bridges from the students' active work to their corresponding work. Most importantly, students should frequently reflect on their actions in relation to the mathematical concepts the teacher is promoting and the constraints of the task as they conceive it.

Despite the known benefits of hands-on learning, many mathematics teachers do not take full advantage of this strategy's effectiveness for learning. Although most mathematics teachers have access to a variety of manipulatives such as Play-Doh, algebra and geometry tiles, and interactive, virtual manipulatives, they incorporate them into their lessons with varying frequency, if at all.

Implications to Think About

The kinds of experiences teachers provide play a major role in the extent and quality of student learning. Students' understanding will increase if they are actively engaged in tasks and experiences designed to deepen and connect their knowledge of mathematical concepts. Individual students learn in different ways. Through the use of manipulatives, various senses are brought into play. When students can touch and move objects to make visual representation of mathematical concepts, different learning modalities are addressed.

No single best method exists for mathematics instruction. However, we do know that any mathematics topic should involve multiple instructional techniques, allowing all students to develop a mathematical understanding. For example, by presenting an activity with three components (manipulatives, technology, and formalizing), we not only give students with varied learning styles different ways to see a problem, we also give them extra time to process the concept.

Using manipulatives in combination with other hands-on instructional methods can enrich and deepen students' understanding. Appropriate use of concrete materials should be one component of a comprehensive mathematics education program.

Resources for Learning More

CompassLearning. (2009). *Professional development.*

Freer Weiss, D. M. (2006, January). "Keeping it real: The rationale for using manipulatives in the middle grades."

Johnson, J. (2000). *Teaching and learning mathematics: Using research to shift from the "yesterday" mind to the "tomorrow" mind.*

Moyer, P. S., Bolyard, J. J., & Spikell, M. A. (2002, February). "What are virtual manipulatives?"

National Council of Teachers of Mathematics. (2000). *Principles and standards for school mathematics.*

Oliva, M. (2005). *NCLB implementation center, building capacity through high-quality teachers: A literature review on recruiting and retaining high-quality teachers.*

Schackow, J. B. (2006). "Using virtual manipulatives to model computation with fractions."

Sowell, E. J. (1989). "Effects of manipulative materials in mathematics instruction."

Suh, J., & Moyer, P. S. (2007). "Developing students' representational fluency using virtual and physical algebra balances."

Utah State University. (2009). *National Library of Virtual Manipulatives.*

6

How does using contextual or applied activities improve student learning in mathematics?

Research and Ideas to Know About

Teachers have long thought that classroom activities with application to real-world situations are the lessons students learn from and appreciate the most. Students have more meaningful learning experiences when mathematical concepts have a personal connection to their own lives, beyond a textbook or resource narrative. Today's students, who often are immersed in multimedia environments, are acclimated to multitasking and want to be participants in their learning experiences. Brain research sheds light on why this is the case:

Classroom activities with application to real-world situations are the lessons students seem to learn from and appreciate the most.

- The more senses are used in instruction, the better learners remember, retrieve, and connect information.

- Physical experiences or meaningful contexts provide learners with strong building blocks for knowledge.

- Acquiring new knowledge is enhanced when it is connected to what learners already know.

- Learning is most effective when people engage in "deliberate practice" that includes active monitoring of one's learning.

Information about memory creation and storage, learning, and complex connections helps explain why students learn through hands-on contextual activities. At the elementary level, many teachers use manipulative materials to provide contextual settings. The adage, "I hear and I forget; I see and I remember; I do and I understand," has been a hallmark in elementary education for many years and is supported by brain research.

Older students need similar experiences that involve physical materials or at least real-life contextual settings. Such activities encourage students to be responsible for their learning, to think critically, and to develop as future employees.

By incorporating realistic, integrated, or interdisciplinary activities that build on established knowledge and skills and use more than one sense, memory pathways become more easily accessed and cross-referenced for future use. As the learner ages, the ease of access of learning pathways is directly dependent on stimulation from prior learning. Concepts embedded this way are truly learned. Students learn best when doing.

Implications to Think About

Since hands-on contextual activities help learning, teachers should include them in their lessons. If manipulative materials help illustrate a new concept, use them. Young children may gain a better feeling for place value by chip trading or by exchanging ten blue markers for one red marker or vice versa. Older students may gain a better understanding of solving an algebraic equation by working with manipulatives to physically build a representation of the equation and then solving it through moving the pieces.

Because real-life applied activities help learning, teachers should include a contextual setting for many of their lessons. The setting can motivate students to learn the concept or can illustrate the concept. Students' learning may be enhanced if they use their prior knowledge to construct and refine a new concept. For example, students trying to determine which school candidate has the best chance of winning the class presidency can conduct a valid survey by calling upon their knowledge of random sampling and probabilities.

Sources of problem-based learning curricula and authentic assessments are widely available. Real-time data is also available on the Internet. Teachers can develop lessons based on students' interests that naturally make the connections between foundational concepts and an application. Teachers might experiment with interdisciplinary applications as action research projects in the classroom. They can develop a hypothesis for successful impact, implement the lesson, collect data from students' performance, and analyze the data to see if the lesson had the desired result. Understanding the learning process can become a fascinating study for all teachers. As teachers discover the most effective strategies for better student achievement, they can adapt their lessons accordingly.

Resources for Learning More

Bransford, J. D., Brown, A. L., Cocking, R. R., Donovan, M. S., & Pellegrino, J. W. (Eds.). (2000). *How people learn: Brain, mind, experience, and school.*

Lester, F. K. (Ed.). (2007). *Second handbook of research on mathematics teaching and learning.*

McAlonan, S., Hotchkiss, H., & Urich, L. (1999). *Bringing standards to life: A "how to" guide to contextual learning and curriculum integration.*

Sousa, D. A. (2007). *How the brain learns mathematics.*

Williams, D. L. (2007, April). "The what, why, and how of contextual teaching in a mathematics classroom."

6

What can parents do to support student learning in mathematics?

Research and Ideas to Know About

Much research exists on the effectiveness of parental involvement in increasing student achievement. When a school or district implements a well-designed and planned parental involvement effort, all students benefit, regardless of race, ethnicity, or income. Such programs are among the most accurate predictors of student achievement and success.

The National Parent Teacher Association (PTA) recognizes parents as the primary influence in students' lives and as necessary partners in their education. Parental involvement means that a student's parents or guardians participate actively in that child's education. It ranges from volunteering in the classroom to reading with the child before bedtime to assuming leadership roles on school committees.

> Involving parents requires a planned and well-coordinated effort, which takes time.

Parental involvement is ineffective when treated as an afterthought. Involving parents requires a planned and well-coordinated effort, which takes time and may not be a priority. A well-designed program provides many benefits: higher grades; better attendance; increased motivation; improved self-esteem; consistent completion of homework; higher graduation rates; decreased alcohol use, violence, and antisocial behavior; and greater support and ratings of teachers by parents and community.

Successful parental involvement programs contain components that represent best practices and are addressed in the National PTA's (2009) standards:

- *Welcoming all families into the school community*—Families are active participants in the life of the school, and feel welcomed, valued, and connected to each other, to school staff, and to what students are learning and doing in class.

- *Communicating effectively*—Families and school staff engage in regular, two-way, meaningful communication about student learning.

- *Supporting student success*—Families and school staff continuously collaborate to support students' learning and healthy development both at home and at school, and have regular opportunities to strengthen their knowledge and skills to do so effectively.

- *Speaking up for every child*—Families are empowered to be advocates for their own and other children, to ensure that students are treated fairly and have access to learning opportunities that will support their success.

- *Sharing power*—Families and school staff are equal partners in decisions that affect children and families and together inform, influence, and create policies, practices, and programs.

- *Collaborating with community*—Families and school staff collaborate with community members to connect students, families, and staff to expanded learning opportunities, community services, and civic participation.

These standards assist educators, parents, and the community in developing or improving parental involvement programs within the context of locally identified needs.

Implications to Think About

Parents and children can enjoy mathematics together. With the proper resources and information, parents, families, and the community can become a teacher's greatest asset and support system.

Schools should begin communicating with parents early in the school year. Although most schools have open houses, a school could give parents an orientation to all opportunities available throughout the school year, including a brief introduction to standards, how parents can contact school staff and administration if they have concerns, and how different subjects are taught.

The EQUALS and FAMILY MATH website has excellent programs that show parents how to encourage mathematics learning and problem solving. The U.S. Department of Education and the National Science Foundation publish free parent resources that schools can send home with children. Schools using a nontraditional mathematics program can involve parents in the activities their child is learning, thus illustrating the mathematics content and processes. After this experience, most parents become advocates and spread their enthusiasm to others.

A child is more likely to complete homework when parents find the assignment relevant to their child's education and have assistive guidelines. Many mathematics curricula and programs offer take-home activities and ideas for two-way contact with parents. Teachers can further support student learning by following up with parents about a certain activity.

Volunteering has traditionally meant direct on-site participation, including doing presentations or participating in Career Day. Volunteering could also include activities done at home, however, such as calling Career Day panelists or creating presentation visuals. When alternatives are provided, more parents can participate.

Parents can be vital to decision making and advocacy work for schools, and they can help write proposals for additional funding for school programs. Partnerships enrich educational experiences both in content and context. Schools and local informal education facilities (such as zoos, planetariums, and museums) can codevelop curricula. Community members can be mentors for mathematics careers, and businesses can allow a few hours a year for employed parents to volunteer or attend school conferences.

Resources for Learning More

Burns, M. (2007). *About teaching mathematics: A K–8 resource.*

Fromboluti, C. S., & Rinck, N. (1999, June). *Early childhood: Where learning begins—mathematics.*

Kilpatrick, J., & Swafford, J. (Eds.). (2002). *Helping children learn mathematics.*

Maynard, S., & Howley, A. (1997, June). *Parent and community involvement in rural schools.*

Mirra, A. (Ed.). (2005). *A family's guide: Fostering your child's success in school mathematics.*

National Council of Teachers of Mathematics. (2004). *Figure this! Math challenges for families.*

National Council of Supervisors of Mathematics. (2009). *Report summary service.*

National Parent Teacher Association. (2009). *National standards for family-school partnerships.*

Parker, R. E. (2006). *Supporting school mathematics: How to work with parents and the public.*

Regents of the University of California. (2009). *EQUALS and FAMILY MATH.*

Remillard, J. T., & Jackson, K. (2006). "Old math, new math: Parents' experiences with standards-based reform."

6

What are characteristics of effective homework in mathematics?

Research and Ideas to Know About

Daily, children face the obligatory question from parents: "What did you learn in school today?" The following day, the teacher asks, "Do you have your homework assignment?" Perhaps a better question would be, "What did you learn at home last night?" The home should be a place to extend mathematics learning.

Opinions vary as to homework's positive effect on student achievement. Until recently, homework was a seldom-questioned, long-standing tradition of education. In 2006, Cooper, Robinson, and Patall conducted a meta-analysis to answer the question of homework's effect on student achievement and could not find conclusive evidence. Keeping in mind that this debate exists, we do know that some general characteristics make a homework assignment effective. Homework must emphasize developing students' mathematics skills to solve problems, which will help them understand the world. These mathematics skills are described as "process skills" in *Principles and Standards for School Mathematics* and "habits of mind" in *Benchmarks for Science Literacy*. Studies show a positive correlation between homework and performance on the NAEP tests when teachers assign homework and hold high expectations for student completion.

Homework assignments provide students the opportunity to work on long-term projects that require multiple levels of understanding. Students take ownership when they spend weeks following stock prices in the newspaper, paying close attention to favorites, predicting industry trends, or perhaps even participating in an investment club. Watching TV and timing commercial breaks one night may be interesting, but when students keep data over a few weeks—timing commercials in different types of programs, making charts, and drawing graphs—their learning will go beyond the curriculum.

Homework time is an opportunity for students to reflect on learning and to synthesize their mathematics understandings. Well-designed homework (for example, charting weather patterns) can bring parents and other adults into a student's community of mathematics learners. Assignments should include students discussing their learning with others. This can be done through student learning teams, parental involvement, or teacher-led electronic discussion groups. Teachers should provide students with authentic learning opportunities to experience at home.

> Teachers should provide students with authentic learning opportunities to experience at home.

Implications to Think About

Teachers who value problem-solving skills provide classroom time to develop students' ability to solve problems and assign homework that uses these skills in new settings. Mathematics homework should not be schoolwork done at home; rather, homework should provide opportunities for students to practice skills that have previously been taught, prepare students for new content they will learn, or elaborate on content that has been introduced. The home provides a unique opportunity for students to gain mathematics understanding by solving mathematics problems rather than completing drills for basic skills development.

Teaching for understanding requires carefully designed tasks. Homework assignments should have clear criteria and/or written rubrics that describe expectations and establish student goals. Teachers must be certain that students have access to the materials and resources they will need to complete the assignment. Teachers should also examine all student work.

Homework assignments must be purposeful. Some legitimate purposes for homework include introducing new content, elaborating on information that has already been addressed to deepen students' knowledge, and providing opportunities for students to explore topics of their own interest.

Less is often more when it comes to homework. A product that has been refined by the student results in more effective learning than a large volume of work completed with little thought. The quality of student work is often determined by the standards a teacher sets on the assignment, the time spent reviewing the expectations, and the suggestions for improvements. Selling students on the importance of an assignment as a learning event is important: their ownership will determine the depth and breadth of their learning. However, teachers need to be aware that special circumstances exist for some students and be flexible about the homework due date, while still expecting the work to be completed.

Resources for Learning More

American Association for the Advancement of Science. (1993). *Benchmarks for science literacy.*

Baker, D. P., & LeTendre, G. K. (2005). *National differences, global similarities: World culture and the future of schooling.*

Cooper, H., Robinson, J. C., & Patall, E. A. (2006, Spring). "Does homework improve academic achievement? A synthesis of research, 1987–2003."

Kieff, J. (2007, Spring). "Classroom idea-sparkers."

Loveless, T. (2004). *The 2004 Brown Center report on American education: How well are American students learning?*

Marzano, R. J., & Kendall, J. S. (1996). *A comprehensive guide to designing standards-based districts, schools, and classrooms.*

Marzano, R. J., & Pickering, D. J. (2007, March). "The case for and against homework."

Marzano, R. J., Pickering, D. J., & Pollock, J. E. (2001). *Classroom instruction that works: Research-based strategies for increasing student achievement.*

National Science Foundation. (1999). "Inquiry: Thoughts, views, and strategies for the K–5 classroom."

6

How does teacher learning affect student learning?

Research and Ideas to Know About

One of the strongest predictors of student success is teacher quality. Highly qualified teachers in both mathematics content knowledge and pedagogical skills are more effective. Those who continue to learn deepen their understanding of content applications and knowledge, effective instructional strategies, theoretical bases for instructional decisions, and confidence in decision making. They are more likely to become reflective, competent, professional teachers.

Mathematics teachers who lead students to explore ideas, pose conjectures, and explain their reasoning need robust understanding of the subject. Teachers who use a more inquiry-based approach and who create learning communities need a deep, connected understanding of mathematical concepts in order to facilitate student learning. Comfortable with their own understanding, teachers can anticipate and respond to student misconceptions as well as student insights. Without this understanding, teachers are limited by their own misconceptions, often the same ones entertained by their students. Furthermore, to select mathematical tasks that enable all students to grow mathematically, teachers must realize that students need a deep sense of how each task relates to other tasks, to prior learning, and to future concepts.

Many studies have explored teacher knowledge as evidenced in mathematics achievement tests and formal coursework. More recent studies connect a teacher's knowledge of mathematics and ability to teach mathematics effectively with student achievement. Critical teacher characteristics and behaviors are:

- Well-defined vision of quality mathematics and reflective classroom practices

- Deep understanding of mathematics—concepts, practices, principles, representations, and applications

- Deep understanding of the ways children learn mathematics

- Implementation of methods that draw out and build on student mathematical thinking

- Continual engagement in reflective practice

- Sustained focus on student learning

NCTM's Teaching Principle emphasizes the importance of teacher preparation and continual professional growth for achieving student understanding of mathematics.

> "Teachers need to understand the big ideas of mathematics and be able to represent mathematics as a coherent and connected enterprise. Their decisions and their actions in the classroom—all of which affect how well their students learn mathematics—should be based on this knowledge."
>
> —National Council of Teachers of Mathematics, 2000, p. 17

Implications to Think About

A community of learners includes a teacher who is a learner with students. Mathematics education standards that establish learning goals for students should, and do, expect as much of teachers. When teachers have a deep understanding about the subject matter, they better anticipate and overcome student mathematics misconceptions, and they become more confident about teaching in an inquiry mode. A job-embedded opportunity for such learning occurs while teaching a rich, conceptually based mathematics program. Teachers become both students and teachers of the content. A broad understanding of mathematics provides teachers with a key component for integrating the various strands of mathematics across the curriculum.

Teachers should make decisions based on data; the best data source is the information they gather in the classroom. Teachers who are learners engage in action research to hone their instructional decision-making skills and use the data they collect to adjust their instruction. Teachers and leaders of mathematics instruction should allow time for teachers to practice and reflect on various methods for teaching and representing mathematics content.

Mathematics teachers should stay current in mathematics as well as mathematics education. One way teachers maintain a current knowledge of their content area is through memberships in professional organizations. These organizations provide journals that synthesize current topics in mathematics and mathematics education.

Perhaps the most significant result of teachers being engaged in learning is the enthusiasm for learning they bring to the classroom. Students know when a teacher is excited about learning, which adds to their own interest and enthusiasm for learning.

Resources for Learning More

Cady, J., Meier, S. L., & Lubinski, C. A. (2006, May–June). "Developing mathematics teachers: The transition from preservice to experienced teacher."

Darling-Hammond, L., & Ball, D. L. (1998). *Teaching for high standards: What policymakers need to know and be able to do.*

Johnson, J. (2000). *Teaching and learning mathematics: Using research to shift from the "yesterday" mind to the "tomorrow" mind.*

Ma, L. (1999). *Knowing and teaching elementary mathematics: Teachers' understanding of fundamental mathematics in China and the United States.*

National Council of Supervisors of Mathematics. (2007, Fall). *Improving student achievement by leading sustained professional learning for mathematics content and pedagogical knowledge development.*

National Council of Teachers of Mathematics. (2000). *Principles and standards for school mathematics.*

Wenglinsky, H. (2000). *How teaching matters: Bringing the classroom back into discussions of teacher quality.*

6

References and Resources

Achieve. (2009). *Math works.* Washington, DC: Author.

Adams, T. L., Thangata, F., & King, C. (2005, May). "Weigh" to go! Exploring mathematical language. *Mathematics Teaching in the Middle School, 10,* 444–448.

Adelman, C. (1999). *Answers in the tool box: Academic intensity, attendance patterns, and bachelor's degree attainment.* Washington, DC: U.S. Department of Education.

The Algebra Project. (2009). *The algebra project.* Accessed at www.algebra.org on November 18, 2009.

Allsopp, D., Lovin, L., Green, G., & Savage-Davis, E. (2003, February). Why students with special needs have difficulty learning mathematics and what teachers can do to help. *Mathematics Teaching in the Middle School, 8,* 308–314.

American Association for the Advancement of Science. (1993). *Benchmarks for science literacy.* New York: Oxford University Press.

American Psychological Association. (1997). *Learner-centered psychological principles.* Accessed at www.apa .org/ed/lcp2/lcp14.html on November 12, 2009.

Anderson, R. C., Hiebert, E. H., Scott, J. A., & Wilkinson, I. A. G. (1984). *Becoming a nation of readers: The report of the commission on reading.* Washington, DC: The National Academy of Education.

Apthorp, H. S., Bodrova, E., Dean, C. B., & Florian, J. E. (with Gaddy, B. B., Goodwin, B. R., Lauer, P. A., & Snow-Renner, R.). (2001). *Noteworthy perspectives: Teaching to the core—Reading, writing, and mathematics.* Aurora, CO: Mid-continent Research for Education and Learning.

Armstrong, T. (1994). *Multiple intelligences in the classroom.* Alexandria, VA: Association for Supervision and Curriculum Development.

Armstrong, T. (1998). *Awakening genius in the classroom.* Alexandria, VA: Association for Supervision and Curriculum Development.

Bailey, T. (1998). Integrating vocational and academic education. In Mathematical Sciences Education Board, *High school mathematics at work: Essays and examples for the education of all students* (pp. 24–29). Washington, DC: National Academy Press.

Baker, D. P., & LeTendre, G. K. (2005). *National differences, global similarities: World culture and the future of schooling.* Palo Alto, CA: Stanford University Press.

Ball, D. L., Lubienski, S., & Mewborn, D. (2001). Research on teaching mathematics: The unsolved problem of teachers' mathematical knowledge. In V. Richardson (Ed.), *Handbook of research on teaching* (4th ed., pp. 433–456). Washington, DC: American Educational Research Association.

Banilower, E. R., Boyd, S. E., Pasley, J. D., & Weiss, I. R. (2006). *Lessons from a decade of mathematics and science reform: A capstone report for the local systemic change through teacher enhancement initiative.* Chapel Hill, NC: Horizon Research.

Barber, M., & Mourshed, M. (2007). *How the world's best-performing school systems come out on top.* London: McKinsey & Company.

Barton, M. L., & Heidema, C. (2002). *Teaching reading in mathematics: A supplement to* Teaching reading in the content areas: If not me, then who? (2nd ed.). Alexandria, VA: Association for Supervision and Curriculum Development.

Bass, H. (2003, February). Computational fluency, algorithms, and mathematical proficiency: One mathematician's perspective. *Teaching Children Mathematics, 9,* 322–327.

Battista, M. T. (1994). Teacher beliefs and the reform movement in mathematics education. *Phi Delta Kappan, 75,* 462–470.

Beck, S. (2009). *The good, the bad and the ugly: Or, why it's a good idea to evaluate web sources.* Accessed at http://lib.nmsu.edu/instruction/eval.html on November 18, 2009.

Billmeyer, R., & Barton, M. L. (2002). *Teaching reading in the content areas: If not me, then who?* (2nd ed.). Alexandria, VA: Association for Supervision and Curriculum Development.

Black, P., Harrison, C., Lee, C., Marshall, B., & William, D. (2003). *Assessment for learning: Putting it into practice.* Maidenhead, England: Open University Press.

Blakey, E., & Spence, S. (1990). *Developing metacognition.* Syracuse, NY: ERIC Clearinghouse on Information Resources. (ERIC Document Reproduction Service No. ED327218)

Blythe, T., Allen, D., & Powell, B. S. (1999*). Looking together at student work: A companion guide to assessing student learning.* New York: Teachers College Press.

Boaler, J. (1997). *Experiencing school mathematics: Teaching styles, sex, and setting.* Maidenhead, England: Open University Press.

Bransford, J. D., Brown, A. L., Cocking, R. R., Donovan, M. S., & Pellegrino, J. W. (Eds.). (2000). *How people learn: Brain, mind, experience, and school: Expanded edition.* Washington, DC: National Academy Press.

Bright, G. W., & Joyner, J. M. (Eds.). (1998). *Classroom assessment in mathematics: Views from a National Science Foundation working conference.* New York: University Press of America.

Brodesky, A. R., Gross, F. E., McTigue, A. S., & Tierney, C. C. (2004, October). Planning strategies for students with special needs: A professional development activity. *Teaching Children Mathematics, 11,* 146–154.

Brooks, J. G., & Brooks, M. G. (1993). *In search of understanding: The case for constructivist classrooms.* Alexandria, VA: Association for Supervision and Curriculum Development.

Brown, C. L., Cady, J. A., & Taylor, P. M. (2009, May). Problem solving and the English language learner. *Mathematics Teaching in the Middle School, 14,* 532–539.

Brown, J. E., & Doolittle, J. (2008). *A cultural, linguistic, and ecological framework for response to intervention with English language learners.* Tempe: Arizona State University, National Center for Culturally Responsive Educational Systems.

Brown, J. S., Collins, A., & Duguid, P. (1989, January). Situated cognition and the culture of learning. *Educational Researcher, 18*(1), 32–42.

Bryant, B. R., & Pedrotty Bryant, D. (2008, Winter). Introduction to the special series: Mathematics and learning disabilities. *Learning Disability Quarterly, 31,* 3–8.

Buehl, D. (1998, October). Making math make sense. *WEAC News and Views.* Accessed at www.weac.org/News_and_Publications/education_news/1998-1999/read_math.aspx on November 18, 2009.

Burke, K., & Dunn, R. (2002, Spring). Teaching math effectively to elementary students. *Academic Exchange Quarterly, 6*(1). Accessed at www.rapidintellect.com/AEQweb/mo2105w02.htm on November 17, 2009.

Burke, M. J., & Curcio, F. R. (Eds.). (2000). *Learning mathematics for a new century: 2000 yearbook.* Reston, VA: National Council of Teachers of Mathematics.

Burns, M. (1995). *Writing in math class: A resource for grades 2–8.* Sausalito, CA: Math Solutions.

Burns, M. (2007). *About teaching mathematics: A K–8 resource* (3rd ed.). Sausalito, CA: Math Solutions.

Bush, W. S., & Greer, A. S. (Eds.). (1999). *Mathematics assessment: A practical handbook for grades 9–12.* Reston, VA: National Council of Teachers of Mathematics.

Bush, W. S., & Leinwand, S. (Eds.). (2000). *Mathematics assessment: A practical handbook for grades 6–8.* Reston, VA: National Council of Teachers of Mathematics.

Cady, J., Meier, S. L., & Lubinski, C. A. (2006, May–June). Developing mathematics teachers: The transition from preservice to experienced teacher. *Journal of Educational Research, 99,* 295–306.

Caine, R. N., & Caine, G. (1994). *Making connections: Teaching and the human brain.* Menlo Park, CA: Addison-Wesley.

Campbell, P. B. (1992). *Math, science, and your daughter: What can parents do?* Washington, DC: Office of Educational Research and Improvement, U.S. Department of Education.

Carpenter, T. P., Fennema, E., Franke, M. L., Levi, L., & Empson, S. B. (1999). *Children's mathematics: Cognitively guided instruction.* Portsmouth, NH: Heinemann.

Carpenter, T. P., Levi, L., & Farnsworth, V. (2000, Fall). Building a foundation for learning algebra in the elementary grades. *In Brief, 1*(2), 1–4.

Carroll, W., & Porter, D. (1998). Alternative algorithms for whole-number operations. In L. J. Morrow & M. J. Kenney (Eds.), *The teaching and learning of algorithms in school mathematics: 1998 yearbook* (pp. 106–114). Reston, VA: National Council of Teachers of Mathematics.

Cawelti, G. (Ed.). (2004). *Handbook of research on improving student achievement* (3rd ed.). Alexandria, VA: Educational Research Service.

Chapin, S. H. (2003). *Classroom discussions: Using math talk to help students learn, grades 1–6.* Sausalito, CA: Math Solutions.

Charles, R. I. (2005, Summer). Big ideas and understandings as the foundation for elementary and middle school mathematics. *Journal of Mathematics Education Leadership, 7*(3), 9–24.

Chicago Lesson Study Group. (2009). *Chicago lesson study group.* Accessed at www.lessonstudygroup.net on November 18, 2009.

Clarke, D. (1997). *Constructive assessment in mathematics: Practical steps for classroom teachers.* Emeryville, CA: Key Curriculum Press.

Colburn, W. (2009). *Colburn's first lessons: Intellectual arithmetic, upon the inductive method of instruction.* Ann Arbor: University of Michigan Library.

Collins, A. M. (2000, September 6). Yours is not to reason why. *Education Week, 20*(1), 60.

CompassLearning. (2009). *Professional development.* Accessed at www.compasslearning.com/services/Default.aspx?page=3.0.2 on November 18, 2009.

Cooper, H., Robinson, J. C., & Patall, E. A. (2006, Spring). Does homework improve academic achievement? A synthesis of research, 1987–2003. *Review of Educational Research, 76,* 1–62.

Council of Chief State School Officers. (2009). *Common core state standards initiative.* Accessed at www.ccsso.org/federal_programs/13286.cfm on November 17, 2009.

Cuoco, A. A. (Ed.). (2001). *The roles of representation in school mathematics: 2001 yearbook.* Reston, VA: National Council of Teachers of Mathematics.

Darling-Hammond, L. (1997). *The right to learn: A blueprint for creating schools that work.* San Francisco: Jossey-Bass.

Darling-Hammond, L., & Ball, D. L. (1998). *Teaching for high standards: What policymakers need to know and be able to do* (CPRE Paper No. JRE-04). Philadelphia: University of Pennsylvania, Consortium for Policy Research in Education.

Darling-Hammond, L., & Richardson, N. (2009, February). Teacher learning: What matters? *Educational Leadership, 66*(5), 46–53.

De Corte, E., Greer, B., & Verschaffel, L. (1996). Mathematics teaching and learning. In D. C. Berliner & R. C. Calfee (Eds.), *Handbook of educational psychology* (pp. 491–549). New York: Macmillan.

Dede, C. (2007). Reinventing the role of information and communications technologies in education. In L. Smolin, K. Lawless, & N. C. Burbules (Eds.), *Information and communication technologies: Considerations of current practices for teachers and teacher educators* (Pt. 2, pp. 11–38). Malden, MA: Wiley-Blackwell.

Dewey, J. (1938). *Experience and education.* New York: Collier Books.

Dogan-Dunlap, H. (2004, January). *Changing students' perception of mathematics through an integrated, collaborative, field-based approach to teaching and learning mathematics.* Paper presented at the Joint Mathematics Meetings of the AMS/MAA, Phoenix, AZ.

Dowker, A. (1992, January). Computational estimation strategies of professional mathematicians. *Journal for Research in Mathematics Education, 23*, 45–55.

Driscoll, M. (1999). *Fostering algebraic thinking: A guide for teachers, grades 6–10.* Portsmouth, NH: Heinemann.

Driscoll, M. (with Wing DiMatteo, R., Nikula, J., & Egan, M.). (2007). *Fostering geometric thinking: A guide for teachers, grades 5–10.* Portsmouth, NH: Heinemann.

Duschl, R. A., Schweingruber, H. A., & Shouse, A. W. (Eds.). (2007). *Taking science to school: Learning and teaching sciences in grades K–8.* Washington, DC: National Academies Press.

Education Development Center. (2005). *The K–12 mathematics curriculum center.* Accessed at www2.edc.org/mcc on November 12, 2009.

Education Development Center. (2007). *Addressing accessibility in mathematics.* Accessed at www2.edc.org/accessMath/ on November 12, 2009.

Evan, A., Gray, T., & Olchefske, J. (2006). *The gateway to student success in mathematics and science: A call for middle school reform—the research and its implications.* Washington, DC: American Institutes for Research.

Felder, R. (1996, December). Matters of style. *ASEE Prism, 6*(4), 18–23.

Fennema, E., & Romberg, T. A. (Eds.). (1999). *Mathematics classrooms that promote understanding.* Mahwah, NJ: Lawrence Erlbaum.

Fernandez, C. (n.d.). *Lesson study research group.* Accessed at www.tc.edu/lessonstudy on November 18, 2009.

Fischer, J., & Perez, R. (2008). *Understanding English through mathematics: A research based ELL approach to teaching all students.* San Marcos: Texas State University.

Fisher, D., & Frey, N. (2007). *Checking for understanding: Formative assessment techniques for your classroom.* Alexandria, VA: Association for Supervision and Curriculum Development.

Flores, A. (2007, November). Examining disparities in mathematics education: Achievement gap or opportunity gap? *High School Journal, 91*(1), 29–42.

Foster, G., Sawicki, E., Schaeffer, H., & Zelinski, V. (2002). *I think, therefore I learn!* Markham, Ontario, Canada: Pembroke.

Francis, D. J., Rivera, M., Lesaux, N., Kieffer, M., & Rivera, H. (2006). *Practical guidelines for the education of English language learners: Research-based recommendations for instruction and academic interventions.* Portsmouth, NH: RMC Research Corporation, Center on Instruction.

Frand, J. L. (2000, September/October). The information-age mindset: Changes in students and implications for higher education. *EDUCAUSE Review, 35*(5), 15–24.

Freer Weiss, D. M. (2006, January). Keeping it real: The rationale for using manipulatives in the middle grades. *Mathematics Teaching in the Middle School, 11*, 238–242.

Friedman, M. I., Harwell, D. H., & Schnepel, K. C. (2006). *Effective instruction: A handbook of evidence-based strategies.* Columbia, SC: Institute for Evidence-Based Decision Making in Education.

Froelich, G. W., Bartkovich, K. G., & Foerster, P. A. (1991). *Connecting mathematics: Curriculum and evaluation standards for school mathematics addenda series, grades 9–12.* Reston, VA: National Council of Teachers of Mathematics.

Fromboluti, C. S., & Rinck, N. (1999, June). *Early childhood: Where learning begins—mathematics.* Accessed at www.ed.gov/pubs/EarlyMath/index.html on January 24, 2008.

Fullan, M. G. (2001). *The new meaning of educational change* (3rd ed.). New York: Teachers College Press.

Fuson, K. C. (1992). Research on learning and teaching addition and subtraction of whole numbers. In G. Leinhardt, R. Putnam, & R. A. Hattrup (Eds.), *Analysis of arithmetic for mathematics teaching* (pp. 53–187). Hillsdale, NJ: Lawrence Erlbaum.

Fuson, K. C., Kalchman, M., & Bransford, J. D. (2005). Mathematical understanding: An introduction. In M. S. Donovan & J. D. Bransford (Eds.), *How students learn: Mathematics in the classroom* (pp. 217–256). Washington, DC: National Academies Press.

Gaddy, B. B., Dean, C. B., & Kendall, J. S. (2002). *Noteworthy perspectives: Keeping the focus on learning.* Aurora, CO: Mid-continent Research for Education and Learning.

Gardner, H. (1993). *Multiple intelligences: The theory in practice.* New York: Basic Books.

Garet, M. S., Porter, A. C., Desimone, L., Birman, B. F., & Yoon, K. S. (2001, Winter). What makes professional development effective? Results from a national sample of teachers. *American Educational Research Journal, 38*, 915–945.

Geary, D. C., Boykin, A. W., Embreton, S., Reyna, V., Siegler, R., Berch, D. B., et al. (2008). Report of the task group on learning processes. In National Mathematics Advisory Panel, *Reports of the task groups and subcommittees* (4-i–4-221). Washington, DC: U.S. Department of Education.

Gersten, R., Beckmann, S., Clarke, B., Foegen, A., Marsh, L., Star, J. R., et al. (2009). *Assisting students struggling with mathematics: Response to intervention (RtI) for elementary and middle schools* (NCEE 2009–4060). Accessed at http://ies.ed.gov/ncee/wwc/pdf/practiceguides/rti_math_pg_042109.pdf on September 2, 2009.

Glandfield, F., Bush, W. S., & Stenmark, J. K. (Eds.). (2003). *Mathematics assessment: A practical handbook for grades K–2.* Reston, VA: National Council of Teachers of Mathematics.

Glatthorn, A. (with Bragaw, D., Dawkins, K., & Parker, J.). (1998). *Performance assessment and standards-based curricula: The achievement cycle.* Larchmont, NY: Eye On Education.

Goldberg, P. D., & Bush, W. S. (2003, Fall). Using metacognitive skills to improve 3rd graders' math problem solving. *Focus on Learning Problems in Mathematics, 25*(4). Accessed at http://findarticles.com/p/articles/mi_m0NVC/is_4_25/ai_n6126743/ on November 19, 2009.

Goldsmith, L. T., Mark, J., & Kantrov, I. (2000). *Choosing a standards-based mathematics curriculum.* Portsmouth, NH: Heinemann.

Gonzales, P., Calsyn, C., Jocelyn, L., Mak, K., Kastberg, D., Arafeh, S., et al. (2000). *Pursuing excellence: Comparison of international eighth-grade mathematics and science achievement from a U.S. perspective, 1995 and 1999* (NCES 2001–028). Washington, DC: U.S. Government Printing Office.

Groves, S., & Stacey, K. (1998). Calculators in primary mathematics: Exploring number before teaching algorithms. In L. J. Morrow & M. J. Kenney (Eds.), *The teaching and learning of algorithms in school mathematics: 1998 yearbook* (pp. 120–129). Reston, VA: National Council of Teachers of Mathematics.

Grunow, J. E. (2001). *Planning curriculum in mathematics.* Madison: Wisconsin Department of Public Instruction.

Halpern, D. F., Aronson, J., Reimer, N., Simpkins, S., Star, J. R., & Wentzel, K. (2007). *Encouraging girls in math and science* (NCER 2007–2003). Washington, DC: National Center for Education Research, Institute of Education Sciences, U.S. Department of Education. Accessed at http://ies.ed.gov/ncee/wwc/pdf/practiceguides/20072003.pdf on November 19, 2009.

Hambrick, A., & Svedkauskaite, A. (2005). *Critical issue: Remembering the child: On equity and inclusion in mathematics and science classrooms.* Accessed at www.ncrel.org/sdrs/areas/issues/content/cntareas/math/ma800.htm on January 18, 2008.

Handal, B. (2003). Teachers' mathematical beliefs: A review. *Mathematics Educator, 13*(2), 47–57.

Hellwig, S. J., Monroe, E. E., & Jacobs, J. S. (2000, November). Making informed choices: Selecting children's trade books for mathematics instruction. *Teaching Children Mathematics, 7,* 138–143.

Hembree, R., & Dessart, D. J. (1986, March). Effects of hand-held calculators in precollege mathematics education: A meta-analysis. *Journal for Research in Mathematics Education, 17,* 83–99.

Henningsen, M., & Stein, M. K. (1997, November). Mathematical tasks and student cognition: Classroom-based factors that support and inhibit high-level mathematical thinking and reasoning. *Journal for Research in Mathematics Education, 28,* 524–549.

Heritage, M. (2007, October). Formative assessment: What do teachers need to know and do? *Phi Delta Kappan, 89,* 140–145.

Herman, J. L., & Abedi, J. (2004). *Issues in assessing English language learners' opportunity to learn mathematics* (CSE Report 633). Los Angeles: National Center for Research on Evaluation, Standards, and Student Testing, University of California.

Heuser, D. (2000, January). Mathematics workshop: Mathematics class becomes learner centered. *Teaching Children Mathematics, 6,* 288–295.

Hiebert, J. (1999, January). Relationships between research and the NCTM standards: An introduction. *Journal of Research in Mathematics Education, 30,* 3–19.

Hiebert, J., & Carpenter, T. P. (1992). Learning and teaching with understanding. In D. A. Grouws (Ed.), *Handbook of research on mathematics teaching and learning* (pp. 65–97). New York: Macmillan.

Hiebert, J., Carpenter, T. P., Fennema, E., Fuson, K. C., Wearne, D., Murray, H., et al. (1997). *Making sense: Teaching and learning mathematics with understanding.* Portsmouth, NH: Heinemann.

Hill, H. C., Rowan, B., & Loewenberg Ball, D. (2005, Summer). Effects of teachers' mathematical knowledge for teaching on student achievement. *American Educational Research Journal, 42*, 371–406.

Hill, J. D., & Flynn, K. M. (2006). *Classroom instruction that works with English language learners.* Alexandria, VA: Association for Supervision and Curriculum Development.

Hirsch, C. R. (Ed.). (2007a). *Perspectives on the design and development of school mathematics curricula.* Reston, VA: National Council of Teachers of Mathematics.

Hirsch, C. (with Cox, D., Kasmer, L., Madden, S., & Moore, D.). (2007b, February). Some common themes and notable differences across recent national mathematics curriculum documents. In *K–12 mathematics: What should students learn and when should they learn it?* (pp. 40–51). Arlington, VA: Center for the Study of Mathematics Curriculum.

Hoachlander, G. (1997). Organizing mathematics education around work. In L. A. Steen (Ed.), *Why numbers count: Quantitative literacy for tomorrow's America* (pp. 122–136). New York: College Board.

Horton, R. M., Hedetniemi, T., Wiegert, E., & Wagner, J. R. (2006, April). Integrating curriculum through themes. *Mathematics Teaching in the Middle School, 11*, 408–414.

Hudson, P., & Miller, S. P. (2005). *Designing and implementing mathematics instruction for students with diverse learning needs.* Boston: Allyn & Bacon.

Individuals with Disabilities Education Act Amendments of 1997, Pub. L. No. 105-17, § 1400 *et seq.*, 111 Stat. 37 (1997).

Institute of Education Sciences. (n.d.) *Fast facts.* Accessed at http://nces.ed.gov/fastfacts/display.asp?id=1 on April 28, 2008.

Institute of Education Sciences. (n.d.). *What works clearinghouse.* Accessed at http://ies.ed.gov/ncee/wwc on November 19, 2009.

International Society for Technology in Education. (2007). *National education technology standards for students* (2nd ed.). Eugene, OR: Author.

International Technology Education Association. (2000). *Standards for technological literacy: Content for the study of technology* (3rd ed.). Accessed at www.iteaconnect.org/TAA/PDFs/xstnd.pdf on January 24, 2002.

Jackson, C. K., & Bruegmann, E. (2009). *Teaching students and teaching each other: The importance of peer learning for teachers* (NBER Working Paper 15202). Cambridge, MA: National Bureau of Economic Research. Accessed at www.nber.org/papers/w15202 on September 9, 2009.

Jamison, D. T., Jamison, E. A., Woessmann, L., & Hanushek, E. (2008, Spring). Education and economic growth. *Education Next, 8*(2), 62–70.

Jayanthi, M., Gersten, R., & Baker, S. (2008). *Mathematics instruction for students with learning disabilities or difficulty learning mathematics: A guide for teachers.* Portsmouth, NH: RMC Research Corporation, Center on Instruction.

Jensen, E. (1998). *Teaching with the brain in mind.* Alexandria, VA: Association for Supervision and Curriculum Development.

Johnson, J. (2000). *Teaching and learning mathematics: Using research to shift from the "yesterday" mind to the "tomorrow" mind.* Olympia, WA: Office of the Superintendent of Public Instruction.

Kamii, C., & Dominick, A. (1998). The harmful effects of algorithms in grades 1–4. In L. Morrow & M. J. Kenney (Eds.), *The teaching and learning of algorithms in school mathematics: 1998 yearbook* (pp. 130–140). Reston, VA: National Council of Teachers of Mathematics.

Keleher, L. A. (2006, November). Building a career mathematics file: Challenging students to find the importance of mathematics in a variety of occupations. *Mathematics Teacher, 100*, 292–297.

Kieff, J. (2007, Spring). Classroom idea-sparkers. *Childhood Education, 83*(3), 162-I–162-R.

Kilpatrick, J., Martin, W. G., & Schifter, D. (Eds.). (2003). *A research companion to principles and standards for school mathematics.* Reston, VA: National Council of Teachers of Mathematics.

Kilpatrick, J., & Swafford, J. (Eds.). (2002). *Helping children learn mathematics.* Washington, DC: National Academy Press.

Kilpatrick, J., Swafford, J., & Findell, B. (Eds.). (2001). *Adding it up: Helping children learn mathematics.* Washington, DC: National Academy Press.

Kleiman, G. M. (2004). *What does the research say? Does technology combined with inquiry-based lessons increase students' learning?* Newton, MA: Education Development Center.

Kulm, G., Roseman, J. E., & Treistman, M. (1999, July/August). A benchmarks-based approach to textbook evaluation. *Science Books & Films, 35*(4), 147–153.

Land, S. M., & Greene, B. A. (2000). Project-based learning with the world wide web: A qualitative study of resource integration. *Educational Technology Research and Development, 48*(1), 45–67.

Lawrenz, F., Gravely, A., & Ooms, A. (2006, March). Perceived helpfulness and amount of use of technology in science and mathematics classes at different grade levels. *School Science and Mathematics, 106*, 133.

Lazear, D. (2004). *Higher-order thinking the multiple intelligences way.* Chicago: Zephyr Press.

Leinhardt, G., Zaslavsky, O., & Stein, M. K. (1990, Spring). Functions, graphs, and graphing: Tasks, learning, and teaching. *Review of Educational Research, 60*, 1–64.

Lester, F. K. (Ed.). (2007). *Second handbook of research on mathematics teaching and learning.* Charlotte, NC: Information Age.

Loucks-Horsley, S., Stiles, K., Mundry, S., Love, N., & Hewson, P. W. (1998). *Designing professional development for teachers of science and mathematics.* Thousand Oaks, CA: Corwin Press.

Loveless, T. (2004). *The 2004 Brown Center report on American education: How well are American students learning?* Washington, DC: Brookings Institution Press.

Lubienski, S. T. (2006). Examining instruction, achievement, and equity with NAEP mathematics data. *Education Policy Analysis Archives, 14*(14), 1–33.

Luft, P., Brown, C. M., & Sutherin, L. J. (2007, July/August). Are you and your students bored with the benchmarks? Sinking under the standards? Then transform your teaching through transition! *Teaching Exceptional Children, 39*(6), 39–46.

Ma, L. (1999). *Knowing and teaching elementary mathematics: Teachers' understanding of fundamental mathematics in China and the United States.* Mahwah, NJ: Lawrence Erlbaum.

Maccini, P., & Gagnon, J. C. (2000, January). Best practices for teaching mathematics to secondary students with special needs. *Focus on Exceptional Children, 32*(5), 1–22.

Maccini, P., Mulcahy, C. A., & Wilson, M. G. (2007, February). A follow-up of mathematics interventions for secondary students with learning disabilities. *Learning Disabilities Research & Practice, 22*(1), 58–74.

Martin, T. S. (Ed.). (2007). *Mathematics teaching today: Improving practice, improving student learning* (2nd ed.). Reston, VA: National Council of Teachers of Mathematics.

Marzano, R. J. (2003). *What works in schools: Translating research into action.* Alexandria, VA: Association for Supervision and Curriculum Development.

Marzano, R. J. (2004). *Building background knowledge for academic achievement: Research on what works in schools.* Alexandria, VA: Association for Supervision and Curriculum Development.

Marzano, R. J., & Kendall, J. S. (1996). *A comprehensive guide to designing standards-based districts, schools, and classrooms.* Alexandria, VA: Association for Supervision and Curriculum Development.

Marzano, R. J., Norford, J. S., Paynter, D. E., Pickering, D. J., & Gaddy, B. B. (2001). *A handbook for classroom instruction that works.* Alexandria, VA: Association for Supervision and Curriculum Development.

Marzano, R. J., & Pickering, D. J. (2007, March). The case for and against homework. *Educational Leadership, 6*(64), 74–79.

Marzano, R. J., Pickering, D. J., & Pollock, J. E. (2001). *Classroom instruction that works: Research-based strategies for increasing student achievement.* Alexandria, VA: Association for Supervision and Curriculum Development.

Maynard, S., & Howley, A. (1997, June). *Parent and community involvement in rural schools.* Charleston, WV: ERIC Clearinghouse on Rural Education and Small Schools. (ERIC Document Reproduction Service No. ED408143)

McAlonan, S., Hotchkiss, H., & Urich, L. (1999). *Bringing standards to life: A "how to" guide to contextual learning and curriculum integration.* Denver: Colorado State Department of Education. (ERIC Document Reproduction Service No. ED434885)

McKeachie, W. J. (1995, November). Learning styles can become learning strategies. *National Teaching & Learning Forum, 4*(6). Accessed at www.ntlf.com/html/pi/9511/article1.htm on January 24, 2002.

McMillan, J. H. (Ed.). (2007). *Formative classroom assessment: Theory into practice.* New York: Teachers College Press.

Meier, D. (1995). *The power of their ideas: Lessons for America from a small school in Harlem.* Boston: Beacon Press.

Mewborn, D. S. (2003). Teaching, teachers' knowledge, and their professional development. In J. Kilpatrick, W. G. Martin, & D. Schifter (Eds.), *A research companion to* Principles and standards for school mathematics (pp. 45–52). Reston VA: National Council of Teachers of Mathematics.

Middleton, J. A., & Spanias, P. A. (1999, January). Motivation for achievement in mathematics: Findings, generalizations, and criticisms of the recent research. *Journal for Research in Mathematics Education, 30,* 65–88.

Mirra, A. (2003). *Administrator's guide: How to support and improve mathematics education in your school.* Reston, VA: National Council of Teachers of Mathematics.

Mirra, A. (Ed.). (2005). *A family's guide: Fostering your child's success in school mathematics.* Reston, VA: National Council of Teachers of Mathematics.

Mistretta, R. M. (2005). Integrating technology into the mathematics classroom: The role of teacher preparation programs. *Mathematics Educator, 15*(1), 18–24.

Mokros, J., Russell, S. J., & Economopoulos, K. (1995). *Beyond arithmetic: Changing mathematics in the elementary classroom.* Palo Alto, CA: Dale Seymour.

Morge, S. P. (2007, August). Eliciting students' beliefs about who is good at mathematics. *Mathematics Teacher, 101*, 50–55.

Moschkovich, J., Schoenfeld, A. H., & Arcavi, A. (1993). Aspects of understanding: On multiple perspectives and representations of linear relations and connections among them. In T. A. Romberg, E. Fennema, & T. P. Carpenter (Eds.), *Integrating research on the graphical representation of functions* (pp. 69–100). Hillsdale, NJ: Lawrence Erlbaum.

Moses, R. P., & Cobb, C. E., Jr. (2001). *Radical equations: Math literacy and civil rights.* Boston: Beacon Press.

Moyer, P. S., Bolyard, J. J., & Spikell, M. A. (2002, February). What are virtual manipulatives? *Teaching Children Mathematics, 8*, 372–377.

Mullis, I. V. S., Martin, M. O., Beaton, A. E., Gonzalez, E. J., Kelly, D. L., & Smith, T. A. (1997). *Mathematics and science achievement in the primary school years: IEA's Third International Mathematics and Science Study (TIMSS).* Chestnut Hill, MA: TIMSS International Study Center, Boston College.

Mullis, I. V. S., Martin, M. O., Beaton, A. E., Gonzalez, E. J., Kelly, D. L., & Smith, T. A. (1998). *Mathematics and science achievement in the final year of secondary school: IEA's Third International Mathematics and Science Study (TIMSS).* Chestnut Hill, MA: TIMSS International Study Center, Boston College.

Mullis, I. V. S., Martin, M. O., & Foy, P. (with Olson, J. F., Preuschoff, C., Erberber, E., Arora, A., & Galia, J.). (2008). *TIMSS 2007 international mathematics report: Findings from IEA's Trends in International Mathematics and Science Study at the Fourth and Eighth Grades.* Chestnut Hill, MA: TIMSS & PIRLS International Study Center, Boston College.

Mullis, I. V. S., Martin, M. O., Gonzales, E. J., Gregory, K. D., Garden, R. A., O'Connor, K. M., et al. (2000). *TIMSS 1999 international mathematics report: Findings from IEA's Repeat of the Third International Mathematics and Science Study at the Eighth Grade.* Chestnut Hill, MA: International Study Center, Lynch School of Education, Boston College.

National Assessment of Educational Progress. (2007). *The nation's report card.* Accessed at http://nationsreportcard.gov/math_2007 on January 18, 2008.

National Clearinghouse for English Language Acquisition. (2009). *Frequently asked questions.* Accessed at www.ncela.gwu.edu/faqs/ on November 12, 2009.

National Commission on Excellence in Education. (1983). *A nation at risk: The imperative for educational reform.* Washington, DC: U.S. Government Printing Office.

National Commission on Mathematics and Science Teaching for the 21st Century. (2000). *Before it's too late: A report to the nation from the National Commission on Mathematics and Science Teaching for the 21st Century.* Washington, DC: U.S. Department of Education.

National Council of Supervisors of Mathematics. (2007, Fall). *Improving student achievement by leading sustained professional learning for mathematics content and pedagogical knowledge development* (Position Paper No. 2). Denver, CO: Author.

National Council of Supervisors of Mathematics. (2008a). *PRIME leadership framework.* Denver, CO: Author.

National Council of Supervisors of Mathematics. (2008b, Spring). *Improving student achievement by leading the pursuit of a vision for equity* (Position Paper No. 3). Denver, CO: Author.

National Council of Supervisors of Mathematics. (2008c, Winter). *Improving student achievement in mathematics for students with special needs* (Position Paper No. 4). Denver, CO: Author.

National Council of Supervisors of Mathematics. (2009). *Report summary service.* Accessed at www.mathedleadership.org/OtherResources/rss.html on September 9, 2009.

National Council of Teachers of Mathematics. (1989). *Curriculum and evaluation standards for school mathematics.* Reston, VA: Author.

National Council of Teachers of Mathematics. (1991). *Professional standards for teaching mathematics.* Reston, VA: Author.

National Council of Teachers of Mathematics. (1995). *Assessment standards for school mathematics.* Reston, VA: Author.

National Council of Teachers of Mathematics. (2000). *Principles and standards for school mathematics.* Reston, VA: Author.

National Council of Teachers of Mathematics. (2004). *Figure this! Math challenges for families.* Accessed at www.figurethis.org on November 19, 2009.

National Council of Teachers of Mathematics. (2005, May). *Computation, calculators, and common sense: A position of the National Council of Teachers of Mathematics.* Accessed at www.nctm.org/uploadedFiles/About_NCTM/Position_Statements/computation.pdf on January 23, 2008.

National Council of Teachers of Mathematics. (2006). *Curriculum focal points for prekindergarten through grade 8 mathematics: A quest for coherence.* Reston, VA: Author.

National Council of Teachers of Mathematics. (2008a, March). *The role of technology in the learning and teaching of mathematics: A position of the National Council of Teachers of Mathematics.* Accessed at http://nctm.org/about/content.aspx?id=14233 on April 23, 2008.

National Council of Teachers of Mathematics. (2008b, September). *Teaching mathematics to English language learners: A position of the National Council of Teachers of Mathematics.* Reston, VA: Author.

National Joint Committee on Learning Disabilities. (2005, June). *Responsiveness to intervention and learning disabilities.* Accessed at www.ldaamerica.org/pdf/rti2005.pdf on November 19, 2009.

National Mathematics Advisory Panel. (2008). *Foundations for success: The final report of the National Mathematics Advisory Panel.* Washington, DC: U.S. Department of Education.

National Parent Teacher Association. (2009). *National standards for family-school partnerships.* Accessed at www.pta.org/national_standards.asp on November 18, 2009.

National Research Council. (1989). *Everybody counts: A report to the nation on the future of mathematics education.* Washington, DC: National Academy Press.

National Research Council. (1999). *Designing mathematics or science curriculum programs: A guide for using mathematics and science education standards.* Washington, DC: National Academy Press.

National Research Council. (2000). *Inquiry and the national science education standards: A guide for teaching and learning.* Washington, DC: National Academy Press.

National Research Council. (2004). *Engaging schools: Fostering high school students' motivation to learn.* Washington, DC: National Academies Press.

National Research Council. (2005). *How students learn: History, mathematics, and science in the classroom.* Washington, DC: National Academies Press.

National Science Board. (2008). *Science and engineering indicators 2008* (Vols. 1–2). Arlington, VA: National Science Foundation.

National Science Foundation. (1999). Inquiry: Thoughts, views, and strategies for the K–5 classroom. *Foundations: A monograph for professionals in science, mathematics, and technology education, 2.*

Newman-Gonchar, R., Clarke, B., & Gersten, R. (2009). *A summary of nine key studies: Multi-tier intervention and response to interventions for students struggling in mathematics*. Portsmouth, NH: RMC Research Corporation, Center on Instruction.

North Central Regional Educational Laboratory. (2004). *Connecting with the learner: An equity toolkit* [CD-ROM]. Naperville, IL: Learning Point Associates.

North Central Regional Educational Laboratory. (2005). *Critical Issue: Using technology to improve student achievement*. Accessed at www.ncrel.org/sdrs/areas/issues/methods/technlgy/te800.htm on January 18, 2008.

Oakes, J. (2005). *Keeping track: How schools structure inequality* (2nd ed.). New Haven, CT: Yale University Press.

Oberer, J. J. (2003, Spring). Effects of learning-style teaching on elementary students' behaviors, achievement, and attitudes. *Academic Exchange Quarterly, 7*, 193–199.

O'Donnell, B. D. (2001, April). A personal journey: Integrating mathematics and service learning. *Mathematics Teaching in the Middle School, 6*, 440–446.

Ogle, T., Branch, M., Canada, B., Christmas, O., Clement, J., Fillion, J., et al. (2002). *Technology in schools: Suggestions, tools and guidelines for assessing technology in elementary and secondary education* (NCES No. 2003–313). Washington, DC: National Center for Education Statistics.

Oliva, M. (2005). *NCLB implementation center, building capacity through high-quality teachers: A literature review on recruiting and retaining high-quality teachers*. Naperville, IL: Learning Point Associates.

Organisation for Economic Co-operation and Development. (2004). *Learning for tomorrow's world: First results from PISA 2003*. Paris: Author.

Organisation for Economic Co-operation and Development. (2007). *Education at a glance*. Paris: Author. Accessed at www.oecd.org/document/30/0,3343,en_2649_39263238_39251550_1_1_1_1,00.html on September 9, 2009.

Organisation for Economic Co-operation and Development. (2008). *OECD science, technology and industry outlook*. Paris: Author. Accessed at http://213.253.134.43/oecd/pdfs/browseit/9208101E.PDF on September 9, 2009.

Palacios, L. (2005). *Critical issue: Mathematics education in the era of NCLB—principles and standards*. Accessed at www.ncrel.org/sdrs/areas/issues/content/cntareas/math/ma500.htm on January 18, 2008.

Parker, R. E. (2006). *Supporting school mathematics: How to work with parents and the public*. Portsmouth, NH: Heinemann.

Pashler, H., Bain, P. M., Bottge, B. A., Graesser, A., Koedinger, K., McDaniel, M., et al. (2007). *Organizing instruction and study to improve student learning: A practice guide* (NCER 2007–2004). Accessed at http://ies.ed.gov/ncee/wwc/pdf/practiceguides/20072004.pdf on November 19, 2009.

Payne, R. K. (2005). *A framework for understanding poverty* (Rev. ed.). Highlands, TX: aha! Process.

Paynter, D. E., Bodrova, E., & Doty, J. K. (2005). *For the love of words: Vocabulary instruction that works, grades K–6*. San Francisco: Jossey-Bass.

PBS TeacherLine. (2006). *Developing mathematical thinking with effective questions*. Accessed at http://teacherline.pbs.org/teacherline/resources/questionsheet_vma.pdf on November 19, 2009.

Perkins, I., & Flores, A. (2002, February). Mathematical notations and procedures of recent immigrant students. *Mathematics Teaching in the Middle School, 7*, 346–351.

Philipp, R. A. (2007). Mathematics teachers' beliefs and affect. In F. K. Lester (Ed.), *Second handbook of research on mathematics teaching and learning* (pp. 257–315). Charlotte, NC: Information Age.

Phye, G. D. (Ed.). (1997). *Handbook of academic learning: Construction of knowledge.* New York: Academic Press.

Pitler, H., Hubbell, E. R., Kuhn, M., & Malenoski, K. (2007). *Using technology with classroom instruction that works.* Alexandria, VA: Association for Supervision and Curriculum Development.

Popham, W. J. (2007). *Classroom assessment: What teachers need to know* (5th ed.). Boston: Allyn & Bacon.

Provasnik, S., Gonzales, P., & Miller, D. (2009). *U.S. performance across international assessments of student achievement: Special supplement to the condition of education 2009* (NCES 2009–083). Washington, DC: National Center for Education Statistics, Institute of Education Sciences, U.S. Department of Education.

Pugalee, D. K. (2004, March). A comparison of verbal and written descriptions of students' problem solving processes. *Educational Studies in Mathematics, 55*, 27–47.

Quiroz, P. A., & Secada, W. G. (2003). Responding to diversity. In A. Gamoran, C. W. Anderson, P. A. Quiroz, W. G. Secada, T. Williams, & S. Ashmann, *Transforming teaching in math and science: How schools and districts can support change* (pp. 87–104). New York: Teachers College Press.

Regents of the University of California. (2009). *EQUALS and FAMILY MATH.* Accessed at www.lhs.berkeley.edu/equals on November 19, 2009.

Remillard, J. T., & Jackson, K. (2006). Old math, new math: Parents' experiences with standards-based reform. *Mathematical Thinking & Learning, 8*, 231–259.

Reys, B. J., & Long, V. M. (1995, January). Implementing the professional standards for teaching mathematics: Teacher as architect of mathematical tasks. *Teaching Children Mathematics, 1*, 296–299.

Richard-Amato, P. A., & Snow, M. A. (Eds.). (2005). *Academic success for English language learners: Strategies for K–12 mainstream teachers.* Upper Saddle River, NJ: Pearson Education.

Rigelman, N. R. (2007, February). Fostering mathematical thinking and problem solving: The teacher's role. *Teaching Children Mathematics, 13*, 308.

Roempler, K. S. (2002, July). Search smarter. *ENC Focus, 9*(3), 6–7.

Romagnano, L. (2006). *Mathematics assessment literacy: Concepts and terms in large-scale assessment.* Reston, VA: National Council of Teachers of Mathematics.

Romberg, T. A., & Kaput, J. J. (1999). Mathematics worth teaching, mathematics worth understanding. In E. Fennema & T. A. Romberg (Eds.), *Mathematics classrooms that promote understanding* (pp. 3–17). Mahwah, NJ: Lawrence Erlbaum.

Ronis, D. (2006). *Brain-compatible mathematics* (2nd ed.). Thousand Oaks, CA: Corwin Press.

Rousseau, C., & Tate, W. F. (2003, Summer). No time like the present: Reflecting on equity in school mathematics. *Theory Into Practice, 42*, 210–216.

Rubenstein, R. N. (2007, November). Focused strategies for middle-grades mathematics vocabulary development. *Mathematics Teaching in the Middle School, 13*, 200–207.

Schackow, J. B. (2006). Using virtual manipulatives to model computation with fractions. *On-Math, 5*(1). Accessed at http://my.nctm.org/eresources/toc_onmath.asp?journal_id=6 on January 23, 2008.

Schackow, J. B., & Thompson, D. R. (2005, Fall). High school students' attitudes toward mathematics. *Academic Exchange Quarterly, 9*(3), 12–18.

Schleppegrell, M. J. (2007, April). The linguistic challenges of mathematics teaching and learning: A research review. *Reading & Writing Quarterly, 23,* 139–159.

Schmidt, M. E., & Vandewater, E. A. (2008, Spring). Media and attention, cognition, and school achievement. *Future of Children, 18*(1), 63–85.

Schmidt, W., Houang, R., & Cogan, L. (2002, Summer). A coherent curriculum: The case of mathematics. *American Educator, 26*(2), 10–26.

Schoenfeld, A. H. (2002, January–February). Making mathematics work for all children: Issues of standards, testing, and equity. *Educational Researcher, 31*(1), 13–25.

Schoenfeld, A. H. (2004, January). The math wars. *Educational Policy, 18,* 253–286.

Schrock, K. (2009). *Kathy Schrock's guide for educators.* Accessed at http://school.discoveryeducation.com/schrockguide on November 19, 2009.

Schwartz, S. L. (2005). *Teaching young children mathematics.* Westport, CT: Praeger.

Seki, J. M., & Menon, R. (2007, February). Incorporating mathematics into the science program of students labeled "at-risk." *School Science and Mathematics, 107,* 61.

Senk, S. L., & Thompson, D. R. (Eds.). (2003). *Standards-based school mathematics curricula: What are they? What do students learn?* Mahwah, NJ: Lawrence Erlbaum.

Shafer, M. C., & Romberg, T. A. (1999). Assessment in classrooms that promote understanding. In E. Fennema & T. A. Romberg (Eds.), *Mathematics classrooms that promote understanding* (pp. 159–184). Mahwah, NJ: Lawrence Erlbaum.

Shoshani, Y., & Hazi, R. B. (2007, March). The use of the Internet environment for enhancing creativity. *Educational Media International, 44,* 17–32.

Shulman, L. S. (1986, February). Those who understand: Knowledge growth in teaching. *Educational Researcher, 15*(2), 4–14.

Siegler, R. S., Fristedt, B., Williams, V., Arispe, I., Berch, D. B., & Banfield, M. (2008). Report of the subcommittee on instructional materials. In National Mathematics Advisory Panel, *Reports of the Task Groups and Subcommittees* (pp. 7-i–7-5). Washington, DC: U.S. Department of Education.

Silver, H. F., Strong, R. W., & Perini, M. J. (2000). *So each may learn: Integrating learning styles and multiple intelligences.* Alexandria, VA: Association for Supervision and Curriculum Development.

Slavit, D., & Ernst-Slavit, G. (2007, November). Teaching mathematics and English to English language learners simultaneously. *Middle School Journal, 39*(2), 4–11.

Sleeter, C. E. (2005). *Un-standardizing curriculum: Multicultural teaching in the standards-based classroom.* New York: Teachers College Press.

Smith, M. S. (2001). *Practice-based professional development for teachers of mathematics.* Reston, VA: National Council of Teachers of Mathematics.

Snow-Renner, R., & Lauer, P. A. (2005a). *McREL insights—Professional development analysis.* Aurora, CO: Mid-continent Research for Education and Learning.

Snow-Renner, R., & Lauer, P. A. (2005b). *McREL insights—Standards-based education: Putting research into practice.* Aurora, CO: Mid-continent Research for Education and Learning.

Sousa, D. A. (2005). *How the brain learns* (3rd ed.). Thousand Oaks, CA: Corwin Press.

Sousa, D. A. (2007). *How the brain learns mathematics.* Thousand Oaks, CA: Corwin Press.

Sowell, E. J. (1989). Effects of manipulative materials in mathematics instruction. *Journal for Research in Mathematics Education, 20,* 498–505.

Sparks, D., & Hirsh, S. (1997). *A new vision for staff development.* Alexandria, VA: Association for Supervision and Curriculum Development.

Spoon, J. C., & Schell, J. W. (1998, Winter). Aligning student learning styles with instructor teaching styles. *Journal of Industrial Teacher Education, 35*(2). Accessed at http://scholar.lib.vt.edu/ejournals/JITE/v35n2/ spoon.html on January 24, 2002.

Sprenger, M. (1999). *Learning and memory: The brain in action.* Alexandria, VA: Association for Supervision and Curriculum Development.

Sprenger, M. (2003). *Differentiation through learning styles and memory.* Thousand Oaks, CA: Corwin Press.

Steen, L. A. (1990). *On the shoulders of giants: New approaches to numeracy.* Washington, DC: National Academy Press.

Steffe, L. P., & Wiegel, H. G. (1996). On the nature of a model of mathematical learning. In L. P. Steffe, P. Nesher, P. Cobb, G. A. Goldin, & B. Greer (Eds.), *Theories of mathematical learning* (pp. 477–498). Mahwah, NJ: Lawrence Erlbaum.

Stein, M. K., Remillard, J., & Smith, M. S. (2007). How curriculum influences student learning. In F. Lester (Ed.), *Second handbook of research on mathematics teaching and learning* (pp. 319–370). Greenwich, CT: Information Age Publishing.

Stenmark, J. K. (1989). *Assessment alternatives in mathematics: An overview of assessment techniques that promote learning.* Berkeley: University of California.

Stenmark, J. K., Bush, W. S., & Allen, C. (Eds.). (2001). *Mathematics assessment: A practical handbook for grades 3–5.* Reston, VA: National Council of Teachers of Mathematics.

Stepanek, J., & Jarrett, D. (1997). *Assessment strategies to inform science and mathematics instruction: It's just good teaching.* Portland, OR: Northwest Regional Educational Laboratory.

Stiggins, R. (2004). *Student-involved assessment for learning* (4th ed.). Upper Saddle River, NJ: Prentice-Hall.

Stiggins, R. (2005, December). From formative assessment to assessment for learning: A path to success in standards-based schools. *Phi Delta Kappan, 87,* 324–328.

Stigler, J. W., & Hiebert, J. (1999). *The teaching gap: Best ideas from the world's teachers for improving education in the classroom.* New York: Free Press.

Stigler, J. W., & Hiebert, J. (2004, February). Improving mathematics teaching. *Educational Leadership, 61*(5), 12–17.

Stone, B., & Urquhart, V. (2008). *Remove limits to learning with systematic vocabulary instruction.* Denver, CO: Mid-continent Research for Education and Learning.

Suh, J., & Moyer, P. S. (2007). Developing students' representational fluency using virtual and physical algebra balances. *Journal of Computers in Mathematics and Science Teaching, 26,* 155–173.

Sullivan, P., & Lilburn, P. (2002). *Good questions for math teaching: Why ask them and what to ask, K–6.* Sausalito, CA: Math Solutions.

Svedkauskaite, A., & McNabb, M. (2005). *Critical issue: Multiple dimensions of assessment that support student progress in science and mathematics.* Accessed at www.ncrel.org/sdrs/areas/issues/content/cntareas/science/sc700.htm on January 18, 2008.

Sylwester, R. (1995). *A celebration of neurons: An educator's guide to the human brain.* Alexandria, VA: Association for Supervision and Curriculum Development.

Tarr, J. E., Reys, B. J., Barker, D. D., & Billstein, R. (2006, August). Selecting high-quality mathematics textbooks. *Mathematics Teaching in the Middle School, 12,* 50.

Teachers of English to Speakers of Other Languages. (2006). *PreK–12 English language proficiency standards.* Alexandria, VA: Author.

Teachers of English to Speakers of Other Languages. (2007). *Teachers of English to speakers of other languages.* Accessed at www.tesol.org on November 19, 2009.

Tennison, A. D. (2007, August). Promoting equity in mathematics: One teacher's journey. *Mathematics Teacher, 101,* 28–31.

Thompson, C. L., & Zeuli, J. S. (1999). The frame and the tapestry: Standards-based reform and professional development. In L. Darling-Hammond & G. Sykes (Eds.), *Teaching as the learning profession: Handbook of policy and practice* (pp. 341–375). San Francisco: Jossey-Bass.

Tomlinson, C. A. (1999). *The differentiated classroom: Responding to the needs of all learners.* Alexandria, VA: Association for Supervision and Curriculum Development.

Tomlinson, C. A. (2003). *Fulfilling the promise of the differentiated classroom: Strategies and tools for responsive teaching.* Alexandria, VA: Association for Supervision and Curriculum Development.

Tomlinson, C. A., & McTighe, J. (2006). *Integrating differentiated instruction and understanding by design: Connecting content and kids.* Alexandria, VA: Association for Supervision and Curriculum Development.

Trammel, B. (2001). *Integrated mathematics? Yes, but teachers need support!* Accessed at www.nctm.org/resources/content.aspx?id=1712 on January 23, 2008.

Trends in International Mathematics and Science Study. (2007). *Mathematics achievement of fourth- and eighth-graders between 1995 and 2007.* Accessed at http://nces.ed.gov/timss/results07_math95.asp on August 5, 2009.

Urquhart, V. (2009). *Using writing in mathematics to deepen student learning.* Denver, CO: Mid-continent Research for Education and Learning.

Urquhart, V., & McIver, M. (2005). *Teaching writing in the content areas.* Alexandria, VA: Association for Supervision and Curriculum Development.

U.S. Department of Education. (n.d.). *Doing what works.* Accessed at http://dww.ed.gov on November 19, 2009.

U.S. Department of Education. (2004, March). *Fact sheet: New No Child Left Behind flexibility: Highly qualified teachers.* Accessed at www.ed.gov/nclb/methods/teachers/hqtflexibility.pdf on November 19, 2009.

Utah State University. (2009). *National Library of Virtual Manipulatives.* Accessed at http://nlvm.usu.edu on November 19, 2009.

Valverde, G. A., & Schmidt, W. H. (1997, Winter). Refocusing U.S. math and science education. *Issues in Science and Technology, 14*(2), 60–66.

VanDerHeyden, A. (n.d.). *RTI and math instruction.* Accessed at www.rtinetwork.org/Learn/Why/ar/RTIandMath/1 on November 19, 2009.

van 't Hooft, M., & Swan, K. (Eds.). (2006). *Ubiquitous computing in education: Invisible technology, visible impact.* Mahwah, NJ: Lawrence Erlbaum.

Vierling, L., Frykholm, J., & Glasson, G. (2006, May). Learning mathematics and earth system science . . . via satellite. *Journal of Geoscience Education, 54,* 262–271.

Wallace, F. H., Clark, K. K., & Cherry, M. L. (2006, September). How come? What if? So what? Reading in the mathematics classroom. *Mathematics Teaching in the Middle School, 12,* 108–115.

Walsh, J. A., & Sattes, B. D. (2005). *Quality questioning: Research-based practice to engage every learner.* Thousand Oaks, CA: Corwin Press.

Wenglinsky, H. (2000). *How teaching matters: Bringing the classroom back into discussions of teacher quality.* Princeton, NJ: Milken Family Foundation.

Westwater, A., & Wolfe, P. (2000, November). The brain-compatible curriculum. *Educational Leadership, 58*(3), 49–52.

Williams, D. L. (2007, April). The what, why, and how of contextual teaching in a mathematics classroom. *Mathematics Teacher, 100,* 572–575.

Willoughby, S. S. (2000). Perspectives on mathematics education. In M. J. Burke & F. R. Curcio (Eds.), *Learning mathematics for a new century: 2000 yearbook* (pp. 1–15). Reston, VA: National Council of Teachers of Mathematics.

Winsor, M. S. (2007, December). Bridging the language barrier in mathematics. *Mathematics Teacher, 101,* 372–378.

Wisconsin Department of Public Instruction. (2007). *Adolescent learning toolkit.* Madison, WI: Author.

Wolfe, P. (2001). *Brain matters: Translating research into classroom practice.* Alexandria, VA: Association for Supervision and Curriculum Development.

Wu, H. (1999, Fall). Basic skills versus conceptual understanding: A bogus dichotomy in mathematics education. *American Educator, 23*(3), 50–52.

Ysseldyke, J., & Bolt, D. M. (2007). Effect of technology-enhanced continuous progress monitoring on math achievement. *School Psychology Review, 36,* 453–467.

Zemelman, S., Daniels, H., & Hyde, A. (1998). *Best practice: New standards for teaching and learning in America's schools.* Portsmouth, NH: Heinemann.

Index

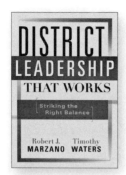

District Leadership That Works
Robert J. Marzano and Timothy Waters

Bridge the divide between administrative duties and daily classroom impact with a leadership mechanism called "defined autonomy." Learn strategies for creating district-defined goals while giving building-level staff the stylistic freedom to respond quickly and effectively to student failure.
BKF314

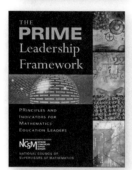

The PRIME Leadership Framework
National Council of Supervisors of Mathematics (NCSM)

Every leader in K–12 mathematics education should own this book. It reveals four leadership principles and twelve action indicators essential to creating equity and excellence in math programs. The NCSM leadership framework for dialogue and collaborative action includes reproducibles, reflective questions, and additional resources.
BKF250

On Excellence in Teaching
Edited by Robert J. Marzano

Learn from the world's best education researchers, theorists, and staff developers. The authors' diverse expertise delivers a wide range of theories and strategies and provides a comprehensive view of effective instruction from a theoretical, systemic, and classroom perspective.
BKF278

Formative Assessment & Standards-Based Grading
Robert J. Marzano

Learn everything you need to know to implement an integrated system of assessment and grading. Marzano explains how to design, interpret, and systematically use three different types of formative assessments and how to track student progress and assign meaningful grades.
BKL003

Ahead of the Curve
Edited by Douglas Reeves

Get the anthology that offers the ideas and recommendations of many of the world's leaders in assessment. Many perspectives of effective assessment design and implementation culminate in a call for redirecting assessment to improve student achievement and inform instruction.
BKF232

Solution Tree | Press

a division of
Solution Tree

Visit solution-tree.com or call 800.733.6786 to order.

Solution Tree | Press

a division of

Solution Tree

Solution Tree's mission is to advance the work of our authors. By working with the best researchers and educators worldwide, we strive to be the premier provider of innovative publishing, in-demand events, and inspired professional development designed to transform education to ensure that all students learn.

Based in Denver, Colorado, McREL (Mid-continent Research for Education and Learning) is a nonprofit organization dedicated to its mission of making a difference in the quality of education and learning for all through excellence in applied research, product development, and service. For more than forty years, McREL has served as the federally funded regional educational laboratory for seven states in the U.S. heartland. Today, it provides services to an international audience of educators. Specifically, it offers a variety of services to help districts translate guidance from this book into results for students. To learn more, contact McREL at 1.800.781.0156 or info@mcrel.org.